"This book could not be more timely, or mc
— *Eileen Fischer, P*
Tanenbaum Chair in Entrepreneurship and Family Enterprise
at Schulich School of Business, Canada

"This is a must read for anyone who wants to be informed about all of the implications of marketing communications, not just the positive contributions of marketing to society otherwise espoused, as well as understand the actions of corporations in and the character and potential future of 'globalized capitalism'. My congratulations to the authors for providing insightful analyses!"
— **Fuat Firat**, *University of Texas, Rio Grande Valley, USA*

"Marketing Communications should be among the most interesting, captivating and intriguing topics of the marketing syllabus but students and scholars alike are often forced to turn to the wider social sciences, media studies and cultural theory to develop thorough and worthwhile insights. In *The Dark Side of Marketing Communications* Hill and McDonagh set out an ambitious and engaging agenda that shows how marketers can engage with some of the most important and topical questions of our times. Despite the critical and at times pessimistic evaluation of the current practices and processes of marketing communications the book suggests that while the Dark Side is certainly powerful and seductive it is also full of contradictions and crisis. This is where we should look for progressive opportunities to develop more sustainable, collective, collaborative and less boringly distracting forms of both marketing and communication."
— **James Fitchett**, *Professor of Marketing and Consumption,*
University of Leicester School of Business, UK

"McDonagh is the master of dark marketing. Hill's a rising star of the same. Individually brilliant, together they're bedazzling. Bright, breezy and bundles of fun, this is the book for you. Especially if you're afraid of the dark."
— **Stephen Brown**, *Professor of Marketing Research,*
Ulster University, UK

THE DARK SIDE OF MARKETING COMMUNICATIONS

What fuels capitalism and what stops it from collapsing? Does marketing communications support and sustain the economic and political status quo?

This book is not about describing the ways in which businesses can optimize the messages they put across or about adding to the marketing communicator's toolkit. It argues that marketing communications plays an increasingly important role in bolstering contemporary capitalism. Drawing on conceptualizations of the 'market' from political economy and sociology, it focusses on five logics that underpin and sustain the form of capitalism in which we live: the logic of competition, the logic of sustainability, the logic of individualism, the logic of objectivity, and the logic of distraction. It does this by exploring those arenas that are increasingly dominated by the communicative activities of business: sport, corporate social responsibility, social media, statistics, and entertainment.

Bringing theories from marketing and consumer research, sociology, cultural studies, and media studies to bear on marketing communications, this book is necessary reading for undergraduate and postgraduate students and academics who wish to understand the broader role of marketing communications in the reproduction of contemporary capitalism.

Tim Hill is Lecturer in Marketing at the University of Bath, UK.

Pierre McDonagh is Professor of Critical Marketing and Society at the University of Bath, UK.

Routledge Studies in Critical Marketing
Edited by Mark Tadajewski and Pauline Maclaran

Marketing has been widely criticised as being probably the least self-critical of all the business disciplines and has never really been able to escape the charge that it is socially, ethically, and morally barren in certain respects. Marketers may talk about satisfying the customer, about building close relationships with their clientele, about their ethical and corporate social responsibility initiatives, but increasingly these claims are subjected to critical scrutiny and been found wanting. In a social, economic, and political environment in which big business and frequently some of the most marketing adept companies' practices are being questioned, there has emerged a very active community of scholars, practitioners and students interested in Critical Marketing Studies.

Using the types of critical social theory characteristic of Critical Marketing Studies, this series will drive the debate on Critical Marketing into the future. It offers scholars the space to articulate their arguments at the level of sophistication required to underscore the contribution of this domain to other scholars, students, practitioners and public-policy groups interested in the influence of marketing in the structuring of the public sphere and society. It is a forum for rigorously theorised, conceptually and empirically rich studies dealing with some element of marketing theory, thought, pedagogy and practice.

Inclusive Place Branding
Critical Perspectives on Theory in Practice
Edited by Mihalis Kavaratzis, Massimo Giovanardi and Maria Lichrou

The Dark Side of Marketing Communications
Critical Marketing Perspectives
Tim Hill and Pierre McDonagh

For more information about the series, please visit https://www.routledge.com/
Routledge-Studies-in-Critical-Marketing/book-series/RSICM

THE DARK SIDE OF MARKETING COMMUNICATIONS

Critical Marketing Perspectives

Tim Hill and Pierre McDonagh

Routledge
Taylor & Francis Group

LONDON AND NEW YORK

First published 2021
by Routledge
2 Park Square, Milton Park, Abingdon, Oxon OX14 4RN

and by Routledge
52 Vanderbilt Avenue, New York, NY 10017

Routledge is an imprint of the Taylor & Francis Group, an informa business

© 2021 Tim Hill and Pierre McDonagh

British Library Cataloguing-in-Publication Data
A catalogue record for this book is available from the British Library

Library of Congress Cataloging-in-Publication Data
Names: Hill, Tim, 1988- author. | McDonagh, Pierre, author.
Title: The dark side of marketing communications : critical marketing
perspectives / Tim Hill, Pierre McDonagh.
Description: New York : Routledge, 2020. | Series: Routledge
studies in critical marketing | Includes bibliographical references
and index.
Identifiers: LCCN 2020022688 (print) | LCCN 2020022689 (ebook) |
ISBN 9781138587120 (hardback) | ISBN 9781138587137 (paperback) |
ISBN 9780429504150 (ebook)
Subjects: LCSH: Capitalism—History—21st century. | Economic
policy—Social aspects.
Classification: LCC HB501.H5173 2020 (print) | LCC HB501 (ebook) |
DDC 658.8/02—dc23
LC record available at https://lccn.loc.gov/2020022688
LC ebook record available at https://lccn.loc.gov/2020022689

ISBN: 978-1-138-58712-0 (hbk)
ISBN: 978-1-138-58713-7 (pbk)
ISBN: 978-0-429-50415-0 (ebk)

Typeset in Bembo
by codeMantra

CONTENTS

ACKNOWLEDGEMENTS

We would like to thank Routledge's Jacqueline Curthoys for initially commissioning this work as well as all of her team who worked on it, especially Emmie Shand. We are beholden to Pauline Maclaran and Mark Tadajewski for their support and encouragement as editors of the Critical Marketing Series as well as our colleagues in the School of Management at the University of Bath.

Pierre thanks his three sons Ethan, Cal, and Dylan Luca for their tolerance as I bored them silly as well as Andy Prothero for her ongoing encouragement and the presence that is Nyko cat. This book is dedicated to my Mum Eileen and Dad, 'Grandad, Desmond, Desie or Des' depending on who is talking to him, I'm proud to be your son and I hope you enjoy the read.

Tim has been sustained by Charlotte, Jo, Les, Arthur the cat, and Marley the dog. Some of these have experienced this book as a collection of bad moods; Marley has experienced the book as a series of long walks.

1

INTRODUCTION

Where are we now?

Hardly more than a quarter-century after Francis Fukuyama (1992) declared 'the end of history', the very countries that advanced liberal democracy and global capitalism have lost confidence in both. In America, protectionism, trade wars, and authoritarianism are the watchwords of the day. The Republican Party rally their base by peddling economic nationalism (Crouch 2018) that allows the Trump administration to withdraw from trade agreements and erect trade barriers (Stiglitz 2018). Meanwhile, Trump's public outbursts of 'spectacular racism', gendered nostalgia, and transgressive vulgarity don't appear to have lost its magic (Hall, Goldstein, and Ingram 2016; Pulido et al. 2019). His campaign for re-election in 2020 will likely parade his unconventional political style, where his exaggerated carnivalesque depictions of his political opponents and marginalized groups again reaffirm that the sun is setting on the political and economic status quo.

In Europe, governments retreat from transnational partnerships. The direction of the United Kingdom's exit from the European Union (EU) is led by politicians enamoured by national mythologies (Thompson 2004) concerning foreign occupation and colonization to champion a 'hard Brexit' (O'Toole 2019). Anti-Semitic conspiracy theories that paint their country as being under perpetual siege by 'globalists' are not just peddled by fringe movements and the marginalized (Drochon 2019) but European governments (Grasseger 2019). Viktor Orbán's use of 'anti-globalist' conspiracy theories to deliver a root-and-branch transformation of Hungarian society serves as a model for other nationalistic politicians (Fabry 2019). After all, the prospect of 'heroic', muscular authoritarian rule is easier to digest if you believe there's a global conspiracy to harm your nation.

Backlash against globalized capitalism is international (Castells 2019; Crouch 2018). The international scale of this malaise shows that it cannot be attributed to the psychological, social, or cultural idiosyncrasies of a single country. This is a deep crisis that goes beyond the antiglobalization movements and anti-capitalist sentiment at the turn of the millennium (Kozinets and Handelman 2004; Kozinets, Handelman, and Lee 2010; Thompson and Arsel 2004; Thompson, Rindfleisch, and Arsel 2006). The clearest indication of globalized capitalism's crisis is the widespread cynicism towards it. Adaptive responses to globalized capitalism have been detailed, for example, through the development of small-scale, local alternative economies (Campana, Chatzidakis, and Laamanen 2017) and social movements and activist groups that take aim at corporations seen to embody the excesses and ills of globalized capitalism (Kozinets and Handelman 2004; Thompson et al. 2006; Varman and Belk 2009). Outside these groups, however, 'exit' and 'voice' responses (Hirschman 1970) now characterize large sections of the Anglo-American-European populations' attitude towards a globalized capitalism and its appointed 'captains' (Bradshaw and Zwick 2016), and dissent is no longer merely expressed by those on the political and social fringes.

Many express the sense that globalized capitalism is unjust, rigged, and unfair. Three-quarters of German adults, two-thirds of Britons, and just over half of Americans believe that "the poor get poorer and the rich get richer in capitalist societies" (YouGov 2015). Surveys examining the extent of conspiracy beliefs show that 44% of British people believe that "even though we live in what's called a democracy, a few people will always run things in this country anyway" (Drochon 2019), a statement that speaks to the extent of systemic inequality rather than the limits of democracy.

The resurgence of 'radical' politics in Europe and America also indicates the extent of backlash against globalized capitalism. In America, the United Kingdom, Italy, Sweden, Hungary, Poland, and the Czech Republic, right-wing nationalist parties have grown in popularity (Muis and Immerzeel 2017; Rooduijn 2015). Simultaneously, once dominant centre-left and social democratic parties have diminished in support (Eaton 2018). Only those parties that have reinvigorated traditional left ideals to combat an increasingly inward-facing and xenophobic right have not suffered humbling defeats at the ballot box (Mouffe 2019).

Champions of science, rationality, and 'the enlightenment' deploy a litany of facts, numbers, and evidence to argue that the world is improving under this socio-economic order (e.g. Pinker 2018). However, these people struggle to justify globalized capitalism's social purpose and moral basis. In the past, defenders of globalized capitalism have explained that it improves the quality of life and working conditions for all (Dunning 2005; Smith 1937). Yet this is no longer the case, and these sorts of justifications are now in short supply. In truth, it is more likely that globalized capitalism is justified on the grounds that 'there is no alternative' (Fisher 2009). Nevertheless, the future of globalized capitalism seems troubled and uncertain.

Our interregnum

To conceptualize this moment, our sense is that globalized capitalism exists in a state of *interregnum* (Fraser 2019; Streeck 2017). This state, Gramsci (1971, 276) writes, witnesses "old is dying and the new cannot be born; in this interregnum a great variety of morbid symptoms appear". Traditionally used to refer to the intermission or handover period between those in electable or heredity positions of power, Gramsci used the term to mark periods of acute uncertainty in which one social order loses its authority at a time where there is nothing yet to replace it (Bauman 2012). Absent an alternative, viable counterhegemonic social order, people face an ongoing political crisis and search for new ideologies and political, cultural, and economic leadership (Fraser 2019).

Variants of capitalism have, of course, recovered through crises previously. It isn't a stretch to suggest that capitalism's durability and strength is derived from its tendencies for self-preservation (Streeck 2017; Wallerstein et al. 2013). Time and time again, capitalism reveals its ability to integrate one-off problems, enduring contradictions, and systemic failures into its own renewal. Dissent is commodified (Frank and Weiland 1997; Heath and Potter 2004; Thompson and Coskuner-Balli 2007), economic and social institutions are transformed to prevent financial bankruptcy (Streeck 2011), and the tendency for declining rates of profit (Marx 1981) is mitigated through expansion into new markets and financialization (Wallerstein et al. 2013). In short, as Streeck (2017, 7) claims, "the history of modern capitalism can be written as a successful of crises that capitalism survive". Nevertheless, while it may be that the ecological and political events of the first two decades of the 21st century may herald nothing more than an intensified and apocalyptic version of globalized capitalism (Noys 2014), it is impossible to say with any certainty or precision what will replace globalized capitalism.

Globalized capitalism's present crisis and its origins

The restructuring of the world economy under globalized capitalism has rewritten the distances between people and places. This is because globalized capitalism is a continual social process of transnational integration through which people connect with dynamic systems of travelling and border-spanning objects, institutions, social practices, and identities (Urry 2003). Marketing and consumer research's predominant concern has been the outcomes of globalization and the various ways in which it has transformed consumer's lives (Askegaard and Kjeldgaard 2007; Ger et al. 2018; Sharifonnasabi, Bardhi, and Luedicke 2019) and, in so doing, has had little say about the forces driving it.

The *causes* and *consequences* of globalization are indissolubly tied to the capitalist dynamics of surplus accumulation (Harvey 2006; Scholte 1997). Capital's demand for accumulation sees no national borders as it seeks to accelerate production, exchange, and consumption through the formation of new overseas markets and location of cheaper labour. As such, globalized capitalism has transformed not only consumer's lives but also how governments and nation states think, operate, and govern. As Alan Greenspan, the former chairman of the Federal Reserve, told a newspaper in 2007, the world was as bankers wanted: "We are fortunate that, thanks to globalization, policy decisions in the U.S. have been largely replaced by global market forces." The brute reality of nation states being subsumed by globalized capitalism has reconfigured relations between politics and economics, with the concerns of the latter trumping the former. It is the prioritization of economics over political power that is partly to blame for global capitalism's problems (Streeck 2017; Tooze 2018; Žižek 2010), a problem that came to head during the global financial crisis (GFC).

Between 2007 and 2012, an economic crisis that started in America had spread, affecting the advanced capitalist societies in East Asia, Russia, and the Eurozone. The conditions of this global crisis were forged through the creation of an international finance system built after the collapse of Bretton Woods system in the 1970s. As Tooze (2018) describes, what emerged in its place was a lightly regulated mishmash system of global financial integration, which left societies vulnerable to any shock in the financial system. In this instance, the drying up of interbank lending caused ripple effects through nations' economies. With banks unable to the secure short-term day-to-day funding on which their existence depended, they ceased to function. On 15 September 2008, Lehmanns filed for bankruptcy, triggering a global panic about the liquidity of the banking system. To stem the crisis, and to confirm economist Robert Skidelsky's adage that "in a crisis, we are all Keynsians", governments intervened in various ways to different effect.

The United States acted globally, with the Federal Reserve going beyond the bailout of their own banks through the provision of liquidity to the European Central Bank and to the Bank of England (Tooze 2018). Crucially, such massive government initiative and intervention was seized upon by the hard-right wing of the Republican Party that framed these actions as another sign of proliferate government spending (Gusterson 2017; Rohlinger and Bunnage 2017). This laid the groundwork for Donald Trump's successful presidential campaign in 2016, and whose reactionary nationalism has seen the United States retreat from global partnerships, use nativist and xenophobic rhetoric to deny recognition and rights, and implement protectionist trade policies (Fraser 2019).

The EU, however, failed to coordinate and assemble a similar intervention. In contrast to the United States's spending, Europeans governments implemented a range of austerity measures (Benmecheddal, Gorge, and Özçağlar-Toulouse 2017; Bradshaw and Ostberg 2019; Roche, O'Connell, and Prothero 2016) to combat plunging tax incomes (Tooze 2018). In the United Kingdom, cuts to social spending hit ex-industrial and heavy-industry communities the hardest, and it is these constituencies that piled behind the 'Leave' vote in the 2017 referendum to leave the EU (Hazeldine 2017). As Hazeldine (2017, 69) sums up, "the rhetoric of Leave was anti-immigrant; the anger that powered it to victory came from decline". Similar dynamics related to economic and geographic inequality can be located in similar political events where pushback against the status quo is a defining feature.

The dark side of marketing communications

Great Financial Crisis

Because of its crucial role in causing this crisis, this book uses the GFC as a historical point to examine how marketing communications sustains the economic and political status quo in the face of this interregnum. We take marketing communications to refer to the process through which any organization works to engage with specific audiences to achieve particular objectives (Fill and Turnbull 2020). Advertisements, CEO speeches, public relations, events, and retail experiences are all tools through which organizations impart their desired message. These messages do not simply seek to persuade, reinforce, and differentiate products and services. These messages also do not merely advance specific representations of class, gender, sexuality, and race (e.g. Borgerson and Schroeder 2002; Bristor, Lee, and Hunt 1995; Crockett 2008; Hirschman 1993, 2003; Stern 1995, 1996), nor do they endow product and services with magical powers that help conceal the inherently political nature of production and consumption (Bradshaw, Campbell, and Dunne 2013; Dholakia 2012). We understand that they also are embedded with interests, values, and logics that sustain the prevailing social order (Hirschman 1993).

This formulation echoes approaches in cultural studies that understands popular culture and media communications as playing a vital role in inducing consent to the dominant social order (Barthes 1956; Hall 1982, 1997; Hebdige 1979). Nike's ideology of hyper-competitive individualism doesn't just resonate with consumers (Holt and Cameron 2010) but also helps naturalize the assertion that people are naturally competitive in ways that help elevate these perspectives into taken-for-granted values. With this ideological approach to marketing communications laid out, this book addresses the how marketing communications are implicated in globalized capitalism's non-death, a slow yet dramatic weakening of the authority of the status quo.

To address the title of the book, for us the 'Dark Side' of marketing communications is not simply that advertisements play a key role in maintaining hierarchies of, for instance, race and gender. To extend and contrast with previous critical approaches, and to speak to the spirit of our time and the historical juncture in which we find ourselves, this book argues that marketing communication's dark side is that it is implicated in the slow, meandering death of a social and economic order that many have lost faith in. Thus, this book sits firmly in the critical tradition for two reasons. First, we are preoccupied with the forces that block, stabilize, and move people, culture, and institutions towards radical, emancipatory, and material change (Held 1990; Murray and Ozanne 1991; Saren et al. 2007). In this sense, we adhere to the spirit of interpretation and transformation that brings together the diversity of thought that comprises critical theory. Second, it seeks to deconstruct the very things we take for granted as being 'normal' as being very contrived (Bouchet 2018; Peñaloza and Barnhart 2011).

One other point of difference is that this book takes more of a 'picaresque' (Black 2016; Robb 2007) turn than is the norm in critical marketing (Saren et al. 2007; Tadajewski 2010a, 2010b). Accordingly, each chapter can be read individually, as a loosely connected episode, or as a whole, in relation to the book's argument. Yet these transgressions with respect to form do not mean we stray away from the aims, norms, and principles that underpin critical marketing specifically and critical theory generally. While no one explicitly wants to play the fool like the carefree libertine André Moreau does as Scaramouche in a perfectly crafted parody of aristocratic consumption as he construes for *Liberté, Equalité, Fraternité*, the values of the French Republic, we point to the need not to self-delude or believe the commercial myths that obscure and hide the pernicious 'dark side' of marketing communications. In this sense we see marketing communications as political and needs to be acknowledged. This book is a small step in that direction.

Critical marketing communications is still formative, but over time it can run the gamut from openly carnivalesque and satirical to feminist, political, socioecological, and philosophical stances to transform critique within the marketing academy and reclaim the megaphone from the broadly functionalist managerialism that dominates its top-tier publications. Certain journals such as *Advertising & Society Review, Consumption Markets & Culture, Journal of Macromarketing, Journal of Consumer Research, Journal of Marketing Management*, and *Journal of Public Policy & Marketing* and *Marketing Theory* have championed criticality to date, but there is still much to be done.

This book contributes to this discussion by arguing that globalized capitalism's captains increasingly look to what marketing communications has to offer in response to the questions, blockages, and doubt, which stem from a political and economic system incapable of breaking out of a cycle of continual crisis. We achieve this by revealing the various ways in which marketing communications helps prop up a socioeconomic system hankering for survival. Accordingly, we show that marketing communications are being used in such a way to express five logics that when taken together constitute an interrelated means for globalized capitalism to temporarily survive. As this book shows, we can sum up that globalized capitalism's 'non-death' rests on its capacity for the relentless production of individuals who see their lives and the social world as fundamentally a *competition*, a world that lauds, celebrates, and makes a virtue out of the struggles against adversity, uncertainty, and precarity. Globalized capitalism must also believe in the system's *sustainability* in the face of climate breakdown and catastrophe. It must therefore make a double move: preventing blame being placed at the door of those principally responsible, while also painting the system as providing the solutions to the climate catastrophe. *Individualism* greases the wheels of consumption in an era where people's existence is graphed now more than any other epoch know to humanity, and where success and status is measured through narcissistic preoccupation with everyday perfection. Globalized capitalism must also be seen as improving the life of those who live in it. While this can be delivered through making material and symbolic improvements to individuals, it is also achieved through widely reported representations of economic and social life (Davies 2018) through GDP and unemployment figures, for instance. But for this to be convincing, not only do the numbers and figures such that represent the system must be positive, but the numbers must be seen as *objective*, unblemished by prejudice, subjectivity, fantasy, or judgement. Finally, globalized capitalism's life depends upon its capacity to *distract* people from the system's most fundamental and systemic problems. In doing so, it prevents people from engaging in politics, in action that strives to reorganize social relations in such a way that does not aim to solely minimize the harms of globalized capitalism but also provides transformative solutions to the problems it has caused.

The book outlined

What are the forces that fuel globalized capitalism and stop it from collapsing immediately? Answering these questions is important if we are to understand how marketing communications exacerbates and sustains the economic, social, and political quo. By drawing on contemporary analyses and theorizations of globalized capitalism across the social sciences and humanities following the GFC, Chapter 2 introduces, describes, and explains five logics that underpin and sustain the specific moment in which we currently live: the logic of competition, the logic of sustainability, the logic of individualism, the logic of objectivity, and the logic of distraction. It is these logics and how they are enforced within elements of society that marketing communications looks to exploit, which is the focus of the chapters that follow.

Chapter 3 answers the question: Why do business leaders and politicians love sport? Why do countries and cities fawn over the Olympics, the Barclays Premier League, or FIFA World Cup? The increased status of sport as a tool for marketing communications following the GFC has been couched within theories of globalization, media, and consumption. We argue that extant theorizations overlook how sport has close ideological affinities with globalized capitalism. In contrast therefore, we explain that sport serves as an icon of globalized capitalism by virtue of how it provides justification for rampant social and economic inequality. With its deserving winners and losers, sport provides moral justification for an economic and political order that increasingly demands that people prove themselves in increasingly different ways relative to one another.

Corporate social responsibility is the topic of Chapter 4. Our argument is not that corporate social responsibility makes business more accountable for their actions, nor is it a method that allows consumers to more easily reward those companies who 'do good'. Rather, this chapter argues that corporate social responsibility's principal aim is to secure trust in our current political and economic leaders with the burden of evading ecological catastrophe. By focusing on a process of legitimation and by drawing upon Galbraith's concept of the techno-structure (Desmond 2003), this chapter reveals how marketing communications are being used to shape a new public discourse around pro-business solutions, sustainable brands, and storytelling of corporate responsibility.

Chapter 5 revisits work concerning possessive individualism, the glue that pervades, grows, and animates the steady growth within advanced capitalist societies. We argue that the pursuit of rational self-interest grounded in the belief that individuals have no ties or responsibilities to others, nor a larger social whole, continues to preclude the formation of alternatives to globalized capitalism.

Objectivity is our consideration in Chapter 6. In an era where the topic of objectivity has been considered by the public through ideas of 'fake news', post-truth, and conspiracy theory (Sismondo 2017; Ylä-Anttila 2018), we examine how objective measures of social progress are subject to criticism. We focus on the example of GDP, which has recently undergone criticism for not reflecting the true nature of society. As one *New York Times* headline put it, "You Can't Feed a Family with GDP". We draw on ideas around the co-production (Jasanoff 2004) of knowledge to explain why it is that GDP has lost its power to represent social progress, and consider the variety of measures champions of globalized capitalism have turned to reclaim their authority.

Distraction forms a key concept in critical theory and is used to explain why and how people remain apoliticized, thus perpetuating the status quo. It is what we consider in Chapter 7. In this chapter, we submit that defining features of distraction has transformed in globalized capitalism. Accordingly, the aim of this chapter is not to add to our understanding that extraordinary, hedonistic experiences provide temporary, restorative relief from the workaday oppression of everyday life. In contrast, this chapter argues that globalized capitalism's world of intensive, information overload, on-demand services, and compulsory digital '24/7' connectivity result in a new form of distraction centred around boredom.

Our afterword invites the reader to engage in the reflexive process of construal, to move beyond marketing managerialism (Delbridge and Keenoy 2010), and to instead locate spaces where alternative economic and social worlds can be born, developed, and implemented. This, the final chapter of the book, sketches out a conceptual and theoretical framework to break out of our interregnum and bring about transformative change at different scales and sizes. It focuses on the repoliticization of consumer subjectivity and the development of social movements, both sources of alternative and radical worlds.

Bibliography

Askegaard, Søren and Dannie Kjeldgaard (2007), "Here, There, and Everywhere: Place Branding and Gastronomical Globalization in a Macromarketing Perspective," *Journal of Macromarketing*, 27(2), 138–47.

Barthes, Roland (1956), *Mythologies*, Paris: Editions du Seuil.

Bauman, Zygmunt (2012), "Times of Interregnum," *Ethics & Global Politics*, 5(1), 49–56.

Benmecheddal, Ahmed, Hélène Gorge, and Nil Özçağlar-Toulouse (2017), "Rethinking Alternative Markets in the Context of Economic Crisis and Austerity in Greece," *Journal of Macromarketing*, 37(2), 193–205.

Black, Donald Taylor (2016), "Culture," in *Austerity and Recovery in Ireland: Europe's Poster Child and the Great Recession*, eds. William K. Roche, Phillip J. O'Connell, and Andrea Prothero, Oxford: Oxford University Press.

Borgerson, Janet L. and Jonathan E. Schroeder (2002), "Ethical Issues of Global Marketing: Avoiding Bad Faith in Visual Representation," *European Journal of Marketing*, 36(5/6), 570–94.

Bouchet, Dominque (2018), "Marketing, Violence and Social Cohesion: First Steps to a Conceptual Approach to the Understanding of the Normalising Role of Marketing," *Journal of Marketing Management*, 34(11–12), 1048–62.

Bradshaw, Alan, Norah Campbell, and Stephen Dunne (2013), "The Politics of Consumption," *Ephemera*, 13(2), 203–16.

Bradshaw, Alan and Jacob Ostberg (2019), "Blaming Consumers: Ideology and European Austerity," *Journal of Consumer Culture*, 19(4), 448–68.

Bradshaw, Alan and Detlev Zwick (2016), "The Field of Business Sustainability and the Death Drive: A Radical Intervention," *Journal of Business Ethics*, 136(2), 267–79.

Bristor, Julia M., Renée Gravois Lee, and Michelle R. Hunt (1995), "Race and Ideology: African-American Images in Television Advertising," *Journal of Public Policy & Marketing*, 14(1), 48–59.

Campana, Mario, Andreas Chatzidakis, and Mikko Laamanen (2017), "Introduction to the Special Issue: A Macromarketing Perspective on Alternative Economies," *Journal of Macromarketing*, 37(2), 125–30.

Castells, Manuel (2019), *Rupture: The Crisis of Liberal Democracy*, Cambridge: Polity Press.

Crockett, David (2008), "Marketing Blackness: How Advertisers Use Race to Sell Products," *Journal of Consumer Culture*, 8(2), 245–68.

Crouch, Colin (2018), *The Globalization Backlash*, New York: Polity Press.

Davies, William (2018), *Nervous States: How Feeling Took Over the World*, London: Jonathan Cape.

Delbridge, Rick and Tom Keenoy (2010), "Beyond Managerialism?," *The International Journal of Human Resource Management*, 21(6), 799–817.

Desmond, John (2003), "Consuming Power," in *Consuming Behavior*, London: Palgrave, 81–136.

Dholakia, Nikhilesh (2012), "Being Critical in Marketing Studies: The Imperative of Macro Perspectives," *Journal of Macromarketing*, 32(2), 220–25.

Drochon, Hugo (2019), "Who Believes in Conspiracy Theories in Great Britain and Europe?," in *Conspiracy Theories & the People Who Believe Them*, ed. Joseph E. Uscomslo, Oxford: Oxford University Press, 337–46.

Dunning, John H. (2005), "Is Global Capitalism Morally Defensible?," *Contributions to Political Economy*, 24, 135–51.

Eaton, George (2018), "Germany's SPD Has Signed Its Death Warrant," *NewStatesman*, https://www.newstatesman.com/politics/staggers/2018/02/germany-s-spd-has-signed-its-death-warrant.

Fabry, Adam (2019), *The Political Economy of Hungary: From State Capitalism to Authoritarian Neoliberalism*, London: Palgrave Pivot.

Fill, Chris and Sarah Turnbull (2020), *Marketing Communications: Discovery, Creation and Conversations*, 7th ed., London: Pearson.

Fisher, Mark (2009), *Capitalist Realism: Is There No Alternative?*, Ropley, Hants: O Books.

Frank, Thomas and Matt Weiland (1997), *Commodify Your Dissent: Salvos from The Baffler*, New York: W.W. Norton.

Fraser, Nancy (2019), *The Old Is Dying and the New Cannot Be Born: From Progressive Neoliberalism to Trumpy and Beyond*, London: Verso.

Fukuyama, Francis (1992), *The End of History and the Last Man*, New York: Free Press.

Ger, Güliz, Eminegül Karababa, Alev Kuruoğlu, Meltem Türe, Tuba Üstüner, and Baskin Yenicioğlu (2018), "Debunking the Myths of Global Consumer Culture Literature," in *The SAGE Handbook of Consumer Culture*, ed. Olga Kravets, Pauline Maclaran, Steven Miles, and Alladi Venkatesh, London: SAGE Publications Ltd, 79–101, http://sk.sagepub.com/reference/the-sage-handbook-of-consumer-culture//i600.xml.

Gramsci, Antonio (1971), *Selections from the Prison Notebooks of Antonio Gramsci*, London: Lawrence and Wishart.

Grasseger, Hannes (2019), "The Unbelievable Story of the Plot Against George Soros," *BuzzFeed News*, https://www.buzzfeednews.com/article/hnsgrassegger/george-soros-conspiracy-finkelstein-birnbaum-orban-netanyahu.

Gusterson, Hugh (2017), "From Brexit to Trump: Anthropology and the Rise of Nationalist Populism: From Brexit to Trump," *American Ethnologist*, 44(2), 209–14.

Hall, Kira, Donna M. Goldstein, and Matthew Bruce Ingram (2016), "The Hands of Donald Trump: Entertainment, Gesture, Spectacle," *HAU: Journal of Ethnographic Theory*, 6(2), 71–100.

Hall, Stuart (1997), *Representation: Cultural Representations and Signifying Practices*, London: SAGE.

—— (1982), "The Rediscovery of Ideology: Return to the Repressed in Media Studies," in *Culture, Society and the Media*, ed. Tony Bennett, James Curran, Michael Gurevitch, and Janet Wollacott, New York: Metheun, 56–90.

Harvey, David (2006), *Spaces of Global Capitalism*, London: Verso.

Hazeldine, Tom (2017), "Revolt of the Rustbelt," *New Left Review*, 105, 51–70.

Heath, Joseph and Andrew Potter (2004), *Nation of Rebels: Why Consumerculture Became Consumer Culture*, New York: HarperBusiness.

Hebdige, Dick (1979), *Subculture: The Meaning of Style*, London: Routledge.

Held, David (1990), *Introduction to Critical Theory: Horkheimer to Habermas*, Cambridge: Polity Press.

Hirschman, Albert O. (1970), *Exit, Voice and Loyalty: Responses to Decline in Firms, Organizations, and States*, Cambridge, MA: Harvard University Press.

Hirschman, Elizabeth C. (1993), "Ideology in Consumer Research, 1980 and 1990: A Marxist and Feminist Critique," *Journal of Consumer Research*, 19(4), 537.

—— (2003), "Men, Dogs, Guns, and Cars--The Semiotics of Rugged Individualism," *Journal of Advertising*, 32(1), 9–22.

Holt, Douglas B. and Douglas Cameron (2010), *Cultural Strategy: Using Innovative Ideologies to Build Breakthrough Brands*, Oxford: Oxford University Press.

Jasanoff, Sheila, Ed. (2004), *States of Knowledge: The Co-Production of Science and Social Order*, London: Routledge.

Kozinets, Robert V. and Jay M. Handelman (2004), "Adversaries of Consumption: Consumer Movements, Activism, and Ideology," *The Journal of Consumer Research*, 31(3), 691–704.

Kozinets, Robert V., Jay M. Handelman, and Michael S. W. Lee (2010), "Don't Read This; or, Who Cares What the Hell Anti-Consumption Is, Anyways?," *Consumption, Markets & Culture*, 13(3), 225–33.

Marx, Karl (1981), *Capital, Volume III*, New York: Vintage.

Mouffe, Chantal (2019), *For a Left Populism*, London: Verso.

Muis, Jasper and Tim Immerzeel (2017), "Causes and Consequences of the Rise of Populist Radical Right Parties and Movements in Europe," *Current Sociology*, 65(6), 909–30.

Murray, Jeff B. and Julie L. Ozanne (1991), "The Critical Imagination: Emancipatory Interests in Consumer Research," *Journal of Consumer Research*, 18(2), 129–44.

Noys, Benjamin (2014), *Malign Velocities: Accelerationism and Capitalism*, Alresford, Hampshire: Zero Books.

O'Toole, Fintan (2019), *Heroic Failure: Brexit and the Politics of Pain*, London: Apollo.

Peñaloza, Lisa and Michelle Barnhart (2011), "Living U.S. Capitalism: The Normalization of Credit/Debt," *Journal of Consumer Research*, 38(4), 743–62.

Pinker, Steven (2018), *Enlightenment Now: The Case for Reason, Science, Humanism, and Progress*, New York: Penguin Books.

Pulido, Laura, Tianna Bruno, Cristina Faiver-Serna, and Cassandra Galentine (2019), "Environmental Deregulation, Spectacular Racism, and White Nationalism in the Trump Era," *Annals of the American Association of Geographers*, 109(2), 520–32.

Robb, David, Ed. (2007), *Clowns, Fools, and Picaros: Popular Forms in Theatre, Fiction and Film*, 43, New York: Brill.

Roche, William K., Philip O'Connell, and Andrea Prothero, eds. (2016), *Austerity and Recovery in Ireland: Europe's Poster Child and the Great Recession*, Oxford: Oxford University Press.

Rohlinger, Deana A. and Leslie Bunnage (2017), "Did the Tea Party Movement Fuel the Trump-Train? The Role of Social Media in Activist Persistence and Political Change in the 21st Century," *Social Media + Society*, 3(2), 205630511770678.

Rooduijn, Matthijs (2015), "The Rise of the Populist Radical Right in Western Europe," *European View*, 14(1), 3–11.

Saren, Michael, Pauline Maclaran, Christina Goulding, Richard Elliott, Avi Shankar, and Miriam Cotterral, eds. (2007), *Critical Marketing: Defining the Field*, London: Routledge.

Scholte, Jan Aart (1997), "Global Capitalism and the State," *International Affairs*, 73(3), 427–52.

Sharifonnasabi, Zahra, Fleura Bardhi, and Marius K. Luedicke (2019), "How Globalization Affects Consumers: Insights from 30 Years of CCT Globalization Research," *Marketing Theory*, 147059311988746. doi: 10.1177/1470593119887469.

Sismondo, Sergio (2017), "Post-Truth?," *Social Studies of Science*, 47(1), 3–6.

Smith, Adam (1937), *The Wealth of Nations*, New York: Random House.

Stern, Barbara B. (1995), "Consumer Myths: Frye's Taxonomy and the Structural Analysis of Consumption Text," *Journal of Consumer Research*, 22(2), 165–85.

——— (1996), "Textual Analysis in Advertising Research: Construction and Deconstruction of Meanings," *Journal of Advertising*, 25(3), 61–73.

Stiglitz, Joseph E. (2018), "Trump and Globalization," *Journal of Policy Modeling*, 40(3), 515–28.

Streeck, Wolfgang (2011), "The Crises of Democratic Capitalism," *New Left Review*, 71(Sept-Oct), 5–29.

——— (2017), *How Will Capitalism End? Essays on a Failing System*, London: Verso.

Tadajewski, Mark (2010a), "Critical Marketing Studies: Logical Empiricism, 'Critical Performativity' and Marketing Practice," *Marketing Theory*, 10(2), 210–22.

——— (2010b), "Towards a History of Critical Marketing Studies," *Journal of Marketing Management*, 26(9–10), 773–824.

Thompson, Craig J. (2004), "Marketplace Mythology and Discourses of Power," *Journal of Consumer Research*, 31(1), 162–80.

Thompson, Craig J. and Zeynep Arsel (2004), "The Starbucks Brandscape and Consumers' (Anticorporate) Experiences of Glocalization," *Journal of Consumer Research*, 31(3), 631–42.

Thompson, Craig J. and Gokcen Coskuner-Balli (2007), "Countervailing Market Responses to Corporate Co-Optation and the Ideological Recruitment of Consumption Communities," *Journal of Consumer Research*, 34(2), 135–52.

Thompson, Craig J., Aric Rindfleisch, and Zeynep Arsel (2006), "Emotional Branding and the Strategic Value of the Doppelgänger Brand Image," *Journal of Marketing*, 70(1), 50–64.Tooze, Adam (2018), *Crashed: How A Decade of Financial Crises Changed the World*, London: Allen Lane.

Urry, John (2003), *Global Complexity*, Cambridge: Polity.

Varman, Rohit and Russell W. Belk (2009), "Nationalism and Ideology in an Anticonsumption Movement," *Journal of Consumer Research*, 36(4), 686–700.

Wallerstein, Immanuel, Randall Collins, Michael Mann, Georgi Drerluguan, and Craig Calhoun (2013), *Does Capitalism Have a Future?*, Oxford: Oxford University Press.

Ylä-Anttila, Tuukka (2018), "Populist Knowledge: 'Post-Truth' Repertoires of Contesting Epistemic Authorities," *European Journal of Cultural and Political Sociology*, 5(4), 356–88.

YouGov (2015), "YouGov/Legatum Institute Survey Results," https://d25d2506sfb94s.cloudfront.net/cumulus_uploads/document/ghloropd9r/Summary_Table.pdf.

Žižek, Slavoj (2010), *Living in the End Times*, London: Verso.

2

DECODING THE MARKET LOGIC

Introduction

Chapter 1 suggested that globalized capitalism is fracturing due to the consequences of the global financial crisis, but there is nothing new that can yet take its place. It is in a state of interregnum, a 'zombified' state (Cronin and Cocker 2019; Gramsci 1971): not alive but also not dead. While there is no sign of a functioning brain, its limbs continue to function, sustaining its partial existence (Peck 2010). Perhaps globalized capitalism's zombified state and partial existence should be of little surprise, since as any aficionado of zombie films can tell you, it is sometimes tougher to kill a zombie than a living person (Fisher 2018). Yet without any sign of a counterhegemonic system appearing on the horizon to replace it, we are left with some questions: what are some of the worldviews, ideals, and practices that business leaders, politicians, and brands have sought to inculcate within society since 2008 to continue to fuel globalized capitalism and stop its immediate collapse? Answering this question requires a consideration of the logics of globalized capitalism in the years following the global financial crisis.

Informed by conceptualizations of globalized capitalism found across economic sociology, cultural studies, and critical theory, this chapter identifies five logics that temporarily sustain this model of shaky social order. We use the term 'logics' deliberately here, but we are hasten to add that we are not talking about the concept of institutional logics (e.g. Durand and Thornton 2018; Ertimur and Coskuner-Balli 2015; Scaraboto and Fischer 2013). The concept of logics to which we refer is more to do with the style of ideological reasoning behind marketing communications (Hirschman 2003; Hirschman and Thompson 1997). As Stuart Hall observed, media can be decoded to get at the 'preferred meaning' of those who made it (cited in Procter 2004, 67). By this, Hall urged critical consideration of what attitudes are being espoused, which behaviours are championed, and what sort of worldviews are being articulated (see also Williamson 1978). Indeed, marketing and consumer research have operated in this cultural studies tradition by drawing on ideas associated with the 'interpretive turn' to locate the rhetorical, mythical, and ideological elements that are carried in advertising (Belk 2017; Hirschman 2003). As a result, research has dispelled the myth that adverts are carriers of perfect and unblemished information (Dunne 2018), but instead has done plenty to explain how advertisements come to embody specific logics that are forged through the appropriation of sound, colour, text, and so on that are assembled in ways that seek to resonate with particular audiences.

The logics we introduce in this chapter comprise competition, sustainability, individualism, objectivity, and distraction. As each chapter of this book subsequently reveals, marketing communications has drawn on each of these logics following the global financial crisis. Before we investigate these logics in greater detail, we first conceptualize globalized capitalism as a diffused yet naturalized set of ideas, norms, and practices through which distances between people and places are rewritten for the purposes of capital accumulation.

What type of thing is globalized capitalism?

To be able to identify the exact nature of globalized capitalism following the global financial crisis, we are sensitive to Foucault's (1980) notion of an apparatus or dispositif. This refers to a set of diffuse yet naturalized set of ideas, norms, and practices through which actors strategically intervene upon to world to shape it. Foucault emphasizes the diffused character of the apparatus:

> What I'm trying to single out with this term is, first and foremost, a thoroughly heterogenous set consisting of discourses, institutions, architectural forms, regulatory statements, philosophical, moral, and philanthropic propositions ... The apparatus itself is the network that can be established between these elements.

This is to say that the crucial point of the apparatus is that because a set of ideas, norms, and practices do not necessarily combine such that it forms a "pure doctrine", the apparatus can nevertheless be identified, treated, and analysed as a coherent object (Gilbert 2013, 7). Indeed, Humphreys and Thompson (2014, 903) explain how, despite the diversity of the apparatus, it nevertheless hangs together, "the actions and outlooks of heterogeneous actors across diverse sites display a tacit coordination because they are operating from a collectively shared understanding and situated within a common historical legacy of rules, regulations, and routines that reflect those understandings". In short, the notion of the apparatus emphasizes how a diverse and heterogeneous set of elements can group together into a common network to deliver strategic outcomes (Rabinow and Rose 2003).

When we speak of globalized capitalism, then, we do from the understanding that it forms an aggregation of ideas, norms, and practices that rewrite distances between people and places for the purposes of capital accumulation (Harvey 2006). Such a process is enabled through remarkable transmutations in technology and science (Castells 2009) that entails fragmentation and decentralization of production across the globe that allow for maximum profit-making opportunities (Robinson 2004). As the airline and automobile industries best demonstrate, the process of manufacturing a plane or a car is now comprised of multiple phases of production found across the world, like a spider's web that stretches across the globe (Dicken 1998). Yet such a process of globalized fragmentation has allowed for the formation of transnational corporations and institutions, whose centralized power stems from their capacity to maintain and spread capitalist market relations intensively and extensively (Kellner 2002; Robinson 2004). In this way, globalized capitalism, through the fragmentation of production globally and the formation of transnational corporations and institutions, integrates countries and regions into a global economy.

As marketing and consumer research explains, globalized capitalism forms a process of transnational integration through which consumers connect with dynamic systems of travelling and border-spanning goods, institutions, logics, social practices, imaginaries, and identities (Beck 2000; Featherstone 1990; Ger et al. 2018; Urry 2003). The benefit of treating globalized capitalism as essentially a process of transnational integration is that it avoids the one-sided moralizing that treats globalized capitalism as a homogenizing, monstrous juggernaut of cultural domination (Ritzer 1996). Instead, the rewriting of distances between people and places simultaneously enables sameness, uniformity, and homogeneity *as well as* difference, hybridization, and heterogeneity (Ger et al. 2018; Sharifonnasabi, Bardhi, and Luedicke 2019). Accordingly, marketing and consumer research has helped describe how globalized capitalism, on the one hand, provides the context through which consumers use transnational, standardized brands as 'commercial passports' (Strizhakova, Coulter, and Price 2008) in ways that create global communities (Cayla and Eckhardt 2008) and, on the other hand, colonizes local markets, threatening traditional ideologies and moralities (Izberk-Bilgin 2012; Varman and Belk 2009), triggering countervailing responses steeped in antiglobalization aesthetics and political stances (Thompson and Arsel 2004). Notwithstanding these practices and outcomes with which consumer research is already familiar, less attention has been paid to the logics through which globalized capitalism has sought to sustain itself since the global financial crisis. In what follows, we identify specific attitudes, behaviours, and worldviews that have been espoused since 2008.

Competition

One logic that forms an essential part of globalized capitalism following the global financial crisis is competition. Competition and capitalism have, since Adam Smith (1937), provided the moral and social justification for markets as a form of social organization. For it is through unrestrained competition, unimpeded by governments, that society is provided with the most efficient al-location of resources (Gane 2020). This is because competition forces producers to not only innovate but also manufacture optimal quantity at the lowest cost, placing downward pressure on prices (Smith 1937). The vision of competition evoked by champions of global capitalism typically centres around entrepreneur-ial ventures. For instance, von Mises (2008, 7) paints a cosy and non-antagonistic picture of competition in entrepreneurial settings, writing that

> If [entrepreneurs] fail to produce in the cheapest and best possible way those commodities which the consumers are asking for most urgently, they suffer losses and are finally eliminated from their entrepreneurial position. Other men who know better how to serve the consumers replace them . . .

However, this image of entrepreneurs competing to secure market demand be-lies the way in which globalized capitalism has moved beyond the reinforcement of the competitive dynamics of markets but to actively introduce competition into new areas of social life since the global financial crisis. Indeed, as Wigger and Busch-Hansen (2013, 604) explain, "The idea that exposure to unrestricted competition brings out the best in human beings, companies, organizations and societies has cast a spell on today's globalized world". Arguably, competition has been elevated from merely a principle of well-functioning markets to a logic that governs and structures everyday social life.

The machinations of post-2008 policymaking in those countries most af-fected by the GFC are those of a system that seeks to inject competition into areas of non-market-based life where there was little previously there. Forms of competitive auditing have proliferated across public and cultural sectors in the United Kingdom as a result of ugly government balance sheets and a belief in the virtues of competition (Davies 2016; Shore and Wright 2015). Regardless of whether it is in higher education or the arts, actors of various sizes compete for limited pools of money and their survival. In a culture that lionizes those at the top, these systems of competitive auditing denounce large swathes of people, organizations, and regions to the status of losers. It is not difficult to see how this logic is played out within contemporary television and film. A look at the Australian hit comedy television series *Winners and Losers* (2011–2016) in which the female protagonists are bound together from the experience of being losers at high school but who are about – at some cost – to become winners celebrates people's dogged, single-minded spirit.

The post-global financial crisis era has also witnessed competitiveness seep into people's sense of self and experience of others. It was Foucault who first recognized a crucial difference in the liberalism of Adam Smith and the variants of neoliberalism spawned across the 20th century: where the former assumes that people are naturally competitive and entrepreneurial, neoliberal thought leaders worked on the assumption that people have a tendency to collaborate and work together (Foucault 2007). As a result, throughout the 20th and 21st centuries, politicians have sought to apply competitive relations throughout all areas of social life (Fisher and Gilbert 2014).

The latter point is crucial, because post-GFC life seems to one where people see living in a society with others as a personal burden, with the existence of others as an encroachment on our personal freedom (Gilbert 2019, 164). Under this condition, social life forms a competitive zero-sum game. Other sick and ill people are competitors for doctors and nurse's attention, and the elderly are pitted against the young 'migrants' versus 'natives' when it comes to public policy. In circumstances where others are treated exclusively as selfish competitors who deplete resources that might otherwise benefit us, a sense of perpetual precarity, insecurity, and isolation reigns (Bardhi and Eckhardt 2017; Rose 2004; Saatcioglu and Ozanne 2013; Streeck 2017). These are socially dangerous conditions that provide a fertile breeding ground for a Nietzchean politics of resentment in which the losers of these zero-sum games are granted victimhood status. These 'silent majorities' serve as a useful tool in political rhetoric across the United States, the United Kingdom, and Australia, populations who often find release in political and cultural leadership that revels in lashing out at their enemies (Engels 2010). Against the backdrop of this logic of competition, people vie for scarce and valuable resources, and whose best bet for succeeding in life is through continued self-optimization, self-help, and proactive entrepreneurialism in all fields of life (Cederström and Spicer 2015; DuFault and Schouten 2020).

Sustainability

The second logic through which globalized capitalism has sought to maintain its legitimacy following the GFC is sustainability. Mann and Wainwright (2019, 78) explain "the historical coincidence of the emergence of global capitalism and the transformation of our planet's atmosphere is no accident". Indeed, globalized capitalism's great strength is its capacity to manufacture 'cheap things' (Patel and Moore 2017) and deliver them around the world. This includes food and energy, as well as televisions, mobile phones, and cars, the latter of which are formed via a network of nation-spanning just-in-time supply chains. Regardless of what is being manufactured, the production, manufacture, delivery, and consumption of the majority of these objects extract carbon and place it in the atmosphere (Moore 2015;). Even with very slow economic growth at the start of the decade caused by the GFC, global carbon emissions for the decades of 2010 and 2020 are likely to be the highest ever recorded (Mann and Wainwright 2019). The consequences of climate change are no longer incomprehensible threats that loom on the horizon, in the distant future, but are having to be faced now, as the Australian bushfires of 2019–2020.

It is against this backdrop that many claim sustainability to be the megatrend of our times (McDonagh and Prothero 2014). Whether you aim to protect the planet or argue for the survival of humans on the planet, sustainability highlights that production and consumption need to become ecologically sustainable or life on the planet may not continue in any tolerable way for humanity. Not only does globalized capitalism rely on nature for its inputs (Moore 2015), it befits those who are front and centre in the system to assure people that the present and future are 'all well' under the status quo (Bradshaw and Zwick 2016). It is in the best interests of the powerful to convince others that they can cope with change and take care of business, even in the face of visible environmental destruction caused by multinational oil corporations (Humphreys and Thompson 2014), and our current reliance on oil more generally. To ignore the challenge of sustainability would imply a naive lack of concern or impotence to act in an ecologically responsible manner.

We submit that marketing communications is used to manage and resolve such anxieties. In much the same way that Brereton (2001) argues for the need to understand and appreciate the social, spatial, and political aesthetics of films, in terms of hopes and fantasies at play, as well as scrutinizing the ideological utopianism which is evident in Hollywood, we stress that business claims concerning their sustainable credentials require careful attention and critical interrogation. Consider, for instance, James Quincey's, Coca-Cola's CEO and Chairman, claims that are accompanied by pristine images of romantic, wild nature (Arnould, Price, and Tierney 1998; Canniford and Shankar 2013),

> Our planet matters. We act in ways to create a more sustainable and better shared future. To make a difference in people's lives, communities and our planet by doing business the right way. We are pleased with our progress against some of our goals, while recognizing that more needs to be done in other areas. We will continue to take action and grow our business the right way—not the easy way. (Coca Cola nd)

In addition, sustainability is deemed important to the future of globalized capitalism because it represents a method to effect its mastery and confers legitimacy and trust in the present system to transmogrify from a state of being non-sustainable to a state of being sustainable (Humphreys and Thompson 2014). Consider the automotive industry's shift from internal combustion engine vehicles to electric vehicles (Martin and Väistö 2016). The internal combustion engine vehicle, most notably the diesel car, is now deemed unhelpful in attempts to be sustainable so drivers globally are being incentivized by manufacturers, governments, and non-government agents to consider buying their newest produced vehicles. Not only does the car industry gain permission to produce vehicles for a mass audience again and manufacturers can compete for market share, but people once again can place their trust in these manufacturers and related systems of expertise (Giddens 1990; Humphreys and Thompson 2014), despite that they previously sold them 'defective' vehicles, ecologically speaking. "Trust is only required where this is ignorance", writes Giddens (1991, 89), and once again marketing communications plays a key role in building trust and confidence in the automotive industry. The result is that it becomes the norm that in 2019 the greenest car available for the individual to own is considered an electric vehicle because the system's figureheads tell people it is and they are happy to be reassured that things are under control and that ecological risk is being mitigated. This is, in a nutshell, Galbraith's notion of 'enlightened self-interest' (1998) with an ecological twist.

Individualism

The third logic through which globalized capitalism has sought to sustain it-self following the GFC is individualism. Individualism is an enduring virtue in market society that dictates that success within globalized capitalism is measured by a person's rise to dizzy heights of wealth and status. Of course, to 'be seen to have done good' has, in recent centuries, always been noteworthy. *The Diaries of Samuel Pepys*, for instance, chronicles conspicuous consumption and all of its wastefulness (Dixon 2001): from displaying their new sartorial choices on Sunday's morning church services to the purchasing of silver plates and jealousy over an abundance of wine in the cellar.

It would be a mistake, however, to draw a line of continuity from 17th-century England to the present day, as to do misses a key transformation in the way in which individualism has been transformed in recent decades. Within more recent globalized capitalism and the hyper-consumption with which it is associated (Killbourne, McDonagh, and Prothero 1997), consumption has lost not only sight of itself but its very foundations – *nature* (Marx 1844; Moore 2015). Indeed, Jameson (1988, 1992) notes how previous forms of capitalism were potentially intelligible to those living in it. However, globalized capitalism's dependencies, relationships, and outcomes are, to a large extent, obscure and unintelligible (Humphreys and Thompson 2014). Accordingly, this means that consumers are either shielded or blind to the impact of their purchases, whether those outcomes be local or remote, localized or distributed.

Accompanying this blindness is the championing of possessive individualism (Macpherson 1962) that sees individualism accomplishment as being tied up to self-ownership, in which they no "bear no positive duties to others, and … almost unfettered discretion over their own labours" (Macpherson 1962, 221). It is a *sine qua non* that to be deemed successful, a person must amass wealth and have power over their own destiny, freedom from the constraints of others, even better if they can also exert influence over others while exercising personal choice. Under a free market this idea is akin to the survival of the fittest. In this case the richest people in society are prevalent and those who thrive under pressure, or excel at competition, are held in high regard. These 'high achievers' are seen by those who are less well off, or perceived as being less worthy, as 'having it all'. In many ways this typifies the move from a more collective way of organizing in society (where 'We' is important) to a more "I" focused society (Held 2006) that lacks empathy and support for the 'undeserving' (Katz 1989), the homeless, unemployed, immigrant, disabled, sick, or dying. This is often characterized in the blockbuster movies which dramatize and laud the successful protagonist and renders invisible the unfortunate person who has not generated wealth or does not yet belong. McDonagh and Brereton (2010) in their analysis of Forbes's Top Ten Business Movies summarize *Citizen Kane* in this regard,

> "No 1. Citizen Kane—Pre-WW2 American zeitgeist. The all-time favorite for film critics across the world, this bravura cinematic tale by the wunderkid of Hollywood, Orson Welles, tells the story of William Randolph Hearst, the media mogul who put together an empire of newspapers, radio stations, magazines, and news services and then built himself the flamboyant monument of San Simeon. As Roger Ebert affirms in his review in the Chicago Sun-Times from May 24, 1998, Hearst was "Ted Turner, Rupert Murdoch, and Bill Gates rolled up into an enigma". He became obsessed with success and "living the American Dream,' ' which affirms that anyone can become successful, if they have the requisite tenacity, conviction, and the entrepreneurial spirit".

Such style of work around wealth is still very much box office material within popular culture and finds voice in television dramas such as *Billions* (2016–to date), where the storyline has Chuck Rhoades as a U.S. Attorney haranguing hedge fund king Bobby "Axe" Axelrod. This is a drama between two powerful New York figures. It is about the hidden connections, backroom deals, and visible 'frontstage' (Goffman 1956) performances between representatives of the contemporary 'power elite' (Mills 1956). Chuck is at the top of the legal profession, Bobby is a figurehead of the finance sector, and the drama transforms the complex and murky interaction between these two areas into a glorified chess match in which Chuck and Bobby attempt to outfox and outsmart each other. *Billions* is an instance of what Bourdieu (1998) termed 'human interest stories', forms of cultural production that depoliticizes, reducing the complexity and politics of what happens in the world to the level of mere battles between individuals. Unfortunately, televisions' power of diffusion means that storylines such as these become dominant ways of seeing and interpreting both financial and legal professions.

Objectivity

The fourth logic through which globalized capitalism has sought to sustain itself following the GFC is objectivity. Those involved in the great projects of modernity have always sought to come to terms with what objective progress may look like and how it may be calculated, represented, and charted over time (Giddens 1990). It is important that these markers of progress are treated as objective, bearing no trace of the creator, unblemished by bias, judgement, or subjectivity (Dalston and Galison 2010). This is knowledge 'purified' of its creation (Canniford and Shankar 2013; Latour 1993). Objective knowledge transcends the individual and stands with a "conquering gaze from nowhere" (Haraway 1988, 581), which promises to make perceptible the previously imperceptible.

Every form and iteration of a market-based society is built on a "rational order of three key components", write Slater and Tonkiss (2001, 26), comprising "the division of labour, commodification, and calculation". In market-based economies then, societal progress has been reduced to mathematics and elaborate forms of economic calculation (Davies 2018; Fırat and Dholakia 2017). And for much of the 20th and 21st centuries, gross domestic product (GDP) was the central calculative measure of societal progress in market-based economies (Hirschman 2016). GDP had God-like status, with presidents and prime ministers taking delight in sharing the improving status of an abstraction called the 'economy'. The assumption was that if GDP was rising, both rich and poor sections of the population were doing better. As the aphorism went, "A rising tide lifts all boats", which worked to justify politicians' prioritization to grow the economy. Yet the GFC has broken once hegemonic measurements of societal progress, such as GDP (Davies 2018).

The charge against GDP is that it is no longer able to reflect the lived economic and social experience of large swaths of American and British populations. In his presidential campaign, Donald Trump was able to rally against the state of the economy even though GDP was rising (Davies 2018). Likewise, claims that the UK economy will suffer as a result of leaving the European Union did not resonate in 2016. Both American and British contexts provide a window into how GDP becomes a useless measure in times of inequality, when economic progress is not distributed equally. As Davies (2018, 76) explains,

> Indicators such as GDP capture things in the aggregate, while GDP per capita captures what this means for people on average. But the divisive effect of economic inequality is such that aggregates and averages are simply no longer credible representations of how things are

Trump's election and Brexit have been framed as a 'win for the proper people' (Runciman 2016). It is easy to see why this populist framing, which pits the 'true people' against the rootless, out-of-touch globally networked cultural and economic 'elite', as resonating for some people (Mazzarella 2019). Across both countries, economic growth and cultural inclusion are unequally distributed. In America, research reveals that between 1978 and 2015 the income of the bottom half of the American population fell by 1%, whereas the income of American population in aggregate rose by 58% during the same period (Alvaredo et al. 2017). Gains in income were heavily distributed by those in the top 10% of earners, who experienced an increase of 115% during this period. In Britain, GDP growth masks the manner in which household wealth decreased in regions of the country such as Yorkshire, which experienced an 8% fall between 2010 and 2015 (Hazeldine 2017). The growth of income in London not only conceals declining income and living standards but also fuels anger and resentment towards metropolitan regions of Britain by those who live in the "places that don't matter" (Rodríguez-Pose 2018).

There is scarcely any surprise that the captains of globalized capitalism would seek to identify new calculative measures that would allow them to retain some degree of authority following the GFC. Environmental concerns *en masse* have led many to rally behind a more nuanced objectivity of the triple bottom line of planet, people, and profit, or to abandon GDP as a measure of social and economic progress altogether (Chatzidakis, Maclaran, and Bradshaw 2012; Lloveras, Quinn, and Parker 2018). We now submit that modernity's 'grand project' against which progress is objectively measured and assessed is now unclear, as globalized capitalism seeks to re-legitimate itself by developing new ways to assess, measure, and understand progress.

Distraction

The fifth logic through which globalized capitalism has sought to sustain itself following the GFC is through providing consumers with more and variegated means to be distracted. This isn't the meaning of distraction Walter Benjamin (1969) had in mind when writing about the way in which people read, interpret, and perceive urban locations (Taussig 1991). In contrast, distraction forms a mechanism by which people avoid placing attention, concentration, and efforts focused on that which truly matters: how to think critically about the oppressive 'sameness' of life, and what it might be to live otherwise (Held 1990; Horkheimer and Adorno 1996).

Extraordinary experiences, holidays, new fitness regimes, minute-by-minute news, the latest quiz, the latest podcast, and the latest radical technology – these not only distract from any real, material social issues but also preserve dominant social and economic relations; they distract from boredom. They distract from the drudgery of everyday life and a routine working week. They distract from immediate pressing political and social tasks and the spectre of a climate crisis. What is distracting continues to change, in intensity and in variety, fuelled by the competitive landscape provided by the 'experience economy' (Pine and Gilmore 2011). To this end, globalized capitalism concocts more ways for consumers to amuse themselves, to temporarily escape, and to sense that they are consuming "something metaphysically meaningful, somewhere the spontaneity of life is being restored" (Adorno 2001, 158).

Initially used by Horkheimer and Adorno to describe how the mass media simultaneously entertains while changing nothing, distraction has provided a useful explanation for why and how people remain apolitical, numb to the world around them. Horkheimer and Adorno (1996) attributed the production of distractions to the 'culture industry' that formed the mass media and commercial entertainment industry of the mid- to late 20th century: music, film, television, and magazines. For Adorno especially, the problem of these lay in their relation to the potential for social transformation and political change: "culture now impresses the same stamp on everything. Films, radio and magazines make up a system which is uniform as a whole and in every part" (1996, 120). In short, the culture industry is geared entirely towards the production of content and forms that seek to stabilize the status quo.

Although it would be incorrect to say film, music, and television are the same as they were in the late 20th century, it is possible to show that some of the media forms Adorno focused on still work to reproduce dominant worldviews and social and economic relations. The popularity of superhero films demonstrates that the 'goodies', 'baddies', and 'heroes' categories of identifications not only still strike a chord but also provide a formula that continually dominates box offices in the United States. The "spectacular narratives" that underpin superhero films, King (2000, 10) explains, "entail a move toward the imaginary resolution of contradictions that cannot be resolved in reality". Such narratives have been particularly important "in the traumatized post 9/11 climate" (Brown 2017, 2) in which it isn't clear who is the enemy, who is your ally, who is right, who is wrong, and where exactly the next danger will emerge. Superheroes therefore stake a special out a special place in Americans' imagination due to the way in which they can look beyond the curtain to identify the real evildoers and 'save the day'. Although parodies and 'doppelgangers' (Giesler 2012) are emerging in ways that cause Hollywood a few questions, superhero films nevertheless have staying power by virtue of how they ameliorate anxieties that safety, freedom, and peace are precariously at stake in the age of terrorism, and that there is always someone, somewhere, who can take wrestle back control from evil forces. And if you really want to see what really goes into producing the physics defying crusades of superheroes, why not take a look yourself? *Universal Studios* offers a backstage pass to visitors to peek behind curtain of how films are produced. In the 'Exclusive Backlot Access' package, visitors are promised a tour of one of Hollywood's busiest sets. Visitors can exit their special golf buggy like trolley and see what is happening in a working set. They can see the props housed in the *Universal Studio*'s warehouse.

Whereas Adorno focused on astrology and the way in which it promotes individualism as well as reinforcing dependencies on institutions and people outside of our direct control, we can say similar things about another popular form of media entertainment: the lottery. The lottery reflects accurately that the fate of individuals is not tied to their will or their work ethic. It confirms the only way it is possible to become rich is through luck and chance. It suggests that you forget that your life is tied to waged labour and instead put your fate in the hands of luck and chance. If you want to have a happy life, give yourself a chance of striking it rich. Go on, win it even bigger on the EuroMillions, and enter the *Sunday Times* Rich List.

Summarizing how the culture industry is in the game of producing endless distractions, Adorno declared, "it impedes the development of autonomous, independent individuals who judge and decide consciously for themselves" (2005, 106). In this sense, the person of the culture industry is that which is in stark contrast to the person Kant sees as being of the enlightenment, a person who has the courage to reject someone else's authority and instead makes use of their reason to think for themselves (see Foucault 1984). The culture industry is thus 'anti-enlightenment' (Adorno 2005, 106) and appeals to, develops, and reinforces a person's dependencies, precluding any possibility for emancipation. It valorizes obedience, and the distractions the culture industry provides are one of tonics – they keep people going, satiated, and wedded to the status quo. In the chapter on distraction, we identify how globalized capitalism has created a new kind of distraction centred not on providing extraordinary escapes but on an endless stream of low-intensity stimuli to stop us from ever being bored.

Conclusion

These five logics this chapter identified are by no means exhaustive. It would be wrong to suggest otherwise. But these logics are meant to evoke a sense specific attitudes, behaviours, and worldviews have been expressed following the GFC, in advertisements, in public relations, and in the speeches of CEO's and politicians, the majority of which see themselves as champions of globalized capitalism. These logics do not necessarily need to be obvious to those people, brands, and organizations involved in the strategy, design, or delivery of these marketing communications. In each chapter of this book, we return to these logics to examine in greater detail the specific ways in which marketing communications draws on them, encoding them in text, imagery, and sound, and through the narratives they tell.

Bibliography

Adorno, Theodor W. (2001), *The Stars Down to Earth*, London: Routledge.
——— (2005), *The Culture Industry: Selected Essays on Mass Culture*, Florence: Taylor and Francis.
Alvaredo, Facundo, Lucas Chancel, Thomas Piketty, Emmanuel Saez, and Gabriel Zucman (2017), "Global Inequality Dynamics: New Findings from WID.world," *American Economic Review*, 107(5), 404–9.
Arnould, Eric J., Linda L. Price, and Patrick Tierney (1998), "Communicative Staging of the Wilderness Servicescape," *The Service Industries Journal*, 18(3), 90–115.
Bardhi, Fleura and Giana M. Eckhardt (2017), "Liquid Consumption," ed. Eileen Fischer and Deborah J MacInnis, *Journal of Consumer Research*, 44(3), 582–97.
Beck, Ulrich (2000), *What Is Globalization?*, Camb ridge: Polity Press.
Belk, Russell W. (2017), "Qualitative Research in Advertising," *Journal of Advertising*, 46(1), 36–47.
Benjamin, Walter (1969), *The Work of Art in the Age of Mechanical Reproduction*, New York: Schocken Books.
Bourdieu, Pierre (1998), *On Television*, New York: The New Press.
Bradshaw, Alan and Detlev Zwick (2016), "The Field of Business Sustainability and the Death Drive: A Radical Intervention," *Journal of Business Ethics*, 136(2), 267–79.
Brereton, Pat (2001), "Utopian and Fascist Aesthetics: An Appreciation of 'Nature' in Documentary/Fiction Film," *Capitalism, Nature, Socialism*, 12(4), 33–50.
Brown, Jeffrey A. (2017), *The Modern Superhero in Film and Television: Popular Genre and American Culture*, Abingdon, Oxon: Routledge.

Canniford, Robin and Avi Shankar (2013), "Purifying Practices: How Consumers Assemble Romantic Experiences of Nature," *Journal of Consumer Research*, 39(5), 1051–69.

Castells, Manuel (2009), *The Rise of the Network Society*, 1, Second Edition, Oxford: Blackwell.

Cayla, Julien and Giana M. Eckhardt (2008), "Asian Brands and the Shaping of a Transnational Imagined Community," *Journal of Consumer Research*, 35(2), 216–30.

Cederström, Carl and Andre Spicer (2015), *The Wellness Syndrome*, Cambridge: Polity Press.

Chatzidakis, Andreas, Pauline Maclaran, and Alan Bradshaw (2012), "Heterotopian Space and the Utopics of Ethical and Green Consumption," *Journal of Marketing Management*, 28(3–4), 494–515.

Coca Cola (nd), "Sustainable Business | The Coca-Cola Company," https://www.coca-colacompany.com/sustainable-business.

Cronin, James and Hayley L. Cocker (2019), "Managing Collective Effervescence: 'Zomsumption' and Postemotional Fandom," *Marketing Theory*, 19(3), 281–99.

Dalston, Lorraine and Peter Galison (2010), *Objectivity*, Brooklyn, NY: Zone Books.

Davies, William (2016), "The New Neoliberalism," *The New Left Review*, 101(Sept–Oct), 121–34.

———— (2018), *Nervous States: How Feeling Took Over the World*, London: Jonathan Cape.

Dicken, Peter (1998), *Global Shift*, New York: Guilford.

Dixon, Donald F. (2001), "Conspicous Consumption versus the Protestant Ethic: The View from Pepys's Diary," *Journal of Macromarketing*, 21(2), 146–55.

DuFault, Beth Leavenworth and John W. Schouten (2020), "Self-Quantification and the Datapreneurial Consumer Identity," *Consumption Markets & Culture*, 23(3), 1–27.

Durand, Rodolphe and Patricia H. Thornton (2018), "Categorizing Institutional Logics, Institutionalizing Categories: A Review of Two Literatures," *Academy of Management Annals*, 12(2), 631–58.

Engels, Jeremy (2010), "The Politics of Resentment and the Tyranny of the Minority: Rethinking Victimage for Resentful Times," *Rhetoric Society Quarterly*, 40(4), 303–25.

Ertimur, Burçak and Gokcen Coskuner-Balli (2015), "Navigating the Institutional Logics of Markets: Implications for Strategic Brand Management," *Journal of Marketing*, 79(1), 40–61.

Featherstone, Mike (1990), "Global Culture: An Introduction," *Theory, Culture & Society*, 7(2), 1–14.

Fisher, Mark (2018), *K-Punk : The Collection and Unpublished Writings of Mark Fisher (2004–2016)*, London: Repeater Books.

Fisher, Mark and Jeremy Gilbert (2014), *Reclaim Modernity: Beyond Markets, Beyond Machines*, London: Compass.

Fırat, A. Fuat and Nikhilesh Dholakia (2017), "From Consumer to Construer: Travels in Human Subjectivity," *Journal of Consumer Culture*, 17(3), 504–22.Foucault, Michel (1980), "Confessions of the Flesh," in *Power/Knowledge: Selected Interviews and Other Writings*, ed. Colin Gordon, New York: Pantheon, 194–228.

———— (1984), "What Is Enlightenment?," in *The Foucault Reader*, ed. Paul Rabinow, New York: Pantheon Books, 32–50.

———— (2007), *Security, Territory, Population: Lectures at the College De France, 1977–78*, London: Springer.

Galbraith, John Kenneth (1998), *The Socially Concerned Today*, York, CA: University of Toronto Press.

Gane, Nicholas (2020), "Competition: A Critical History of a Concept," *Theory, Culture & Society*, 37(2), 31–59.

Ger, Güliz, Eminegül Karababa, Alev Kuruoğlu, Meltem Türe, Tuba Üstüner, and Baskin Yenicioğlu (2018), "Debunking the Myths of Global Consumer Culture Literature," in *The SAGE Handbook of Consumer Culture*, London: SAGE Publications Ltd, 79–101, http://sk.sagepub.com/reference/the-sage-handbook-of-consumer-culture//i600.xml.

Giddens, Anthony (1990), *The Consequences of Modernity*, Cambridge: Polity Press.

Giesler, Markus (2012), "How Doppelgänger Brand Images Influence the Market Creation Process: Longitudinal Insights from the Rise of Botox Cosmetic," *Journal of Marketing*, 76(1), 55–68.

Gilbert, Jeremy (2013), "What Kind Of Thing Is 'Neoliberalism'?," *New Formations*, 80(80), 7–22.

——— (2019), "The Joy of Co-production," *IPPR Progressive Review*, 26(2), 161–72.

Goffman, Erving (1956), *The Presentation of Self in Everyday Life*, New York: Doubleday.

Gramsci, Antonio (1971), *Selections from the Prison Notebooks of Antonio Gramsci*, London: Lawrence and Wishart.

Haraway, Donna (1988), "Situated Knowledges: The Science Question in Feminism and the Privilege of Partial Perspective," *Feminist Studies*, 14(3), 575–99.

Harvey, David (2006), *Spaces of Global Capitalism*, London: Verso.

Hazeldine, Tom (2017), "Revolt of the Rustbelt," *New Left Review*, 105, 51–70.

Held, David (1990), *Introduction to Critical Theory: Horkheimer to Habermas*, Cambridge: Polity Press.

Held, Virginia (2006), *The Ethics of Care: Personal, Political, Global*, Oxford: Oxford University Press.

Hirschman, Daniel Abramson (2016), "Inventing the Economy Or: How We Learned to Stop Worrying and Love the GDP," University of Michigan.

Hirschman, Elizabeth C. (2003), "Men, Dogs, Guns, and Cars--The Semiotics of Rugged Individualism," *Journal of Advertising*, 32(1), 9–22.

Hirschman, Elizabeth C. and Craig J. Thompson (1997), "Why Media Matter: Toward a Richer Understanding of Consumers' Relationships with Advertising and Mass Media," *Journal of Advertising*, 26(1), 43–60.

Horkheimer, Max and Theodor W. Adorno (1996), *Dialectic of Enlightenment*, New York: Continuum.

Humphreys, Ashlee and Craig J. Thompson (2014), "Branding Disaster: Reestablishing Trust through the Ideological Containment of Systemic Risk Anxieties," *Journal of Consumer Research*, 41(4), 877–910.

Izberk-Bilgin, Elif (2012), "Infidel Brands: Unveiling Alternative Meanings of Global Brands at the Nexus of Globalization, Consumer Culture, and Islamism," *Journal of Consumer Research*, 39(4), 663–87.

Jameson, Fredric (1988), "Cognitive Mapping," in *Marxism and the Interpretation of Culture*, eds. C Nelson and L Grossberg, Urbana: University of Illinois Press.

——— (1992), *Postmodernism: Or, the Cultural Logic of Late Capitalism*, New York, NY: Verso.

Katz, Michael B. (1989), *The Undeserving Poor: From the War on Poverty to the War on Welfare*, New York: Pantheon Books.

Kellner, Douglas (2002), "Theorizing Globalization," *Sociological Theory*, 20(3), 285–305.

Killbourne, William, Pierre McDonagh, and Andrea Prothero (1997), "Sustainable Consumption and the Quality of Life: A Macromarketing Challenge to the Dominant Social Paradigm," *Journal of Macromarketing*, 17(1), 4–24.

King, Barry (2000), *Spectacular Narratives: Hollywood in the Age of the Blockbuster*, London: I.B. Tauris.

Latour, Bruno (1993), *We Have Never Been Modern*, Harvard University Press.

Lloveras, Javier, Lee Quinn, and Cathy Parker (2018), "Reclaiming Sustainable Space: A Study of Degrowth Activists," *Marketing Theory*, 18(2), 188–202.

Macpherson, Crawford Brough (1962), *The Political Theory of Possessive Individualism: Hobbes to Locke*, Oxford: Clarendon Press.

Mann, Geoff and Joel Wainwright (2019), *Climate Leviathan: A Political Theory of Our Planetary Future*, London: Verso.

Martin, Diane M. and Terhi Väistö (2016), "Reducing the Attitude-Behavior Gap in Sustainable Consumption: A Theoretical Proposition and the American Electric Vehicle Market," in *Marketing in and for a Sustainable Society*, Naresh K. Malhotra, ed., Emerald Group Publishing Limited, 193–213.

Marx, Karl (1844 [1978]), 'Estranged Labour', in *The Marx-Engels Reader*, Second Edition, Robert C. Tucker, ed., New York: W.W. Norton and Company.

Mazzarella, William (2019), "The Anthropology of Populism: Beyond the Liberal Settlement," *Annual Review of Anthropology*, 48(1), annurev-anthro-102218-011412.

McDonagh, Pierre and Andrea Prothero (2014), "Sustainability Marketing Research: Past, Present and Future," *Journal of Marketing Management*, 30(11–12), 1186–1219.

Mills, C. Wright (1956), *The Power Elite*, Oxford: Oxford University Press.

von Mises, Ludwig (2008), *Profit and Loss*, Auburn: Ludwig von Mises Institute.

Moore, Jason W. (2015), *Capitalism in the Web of Life: Ecology and the Accumulation of Capital*, London: Verso.

Patel, Raj and Jason W. Moore (2017), *A History of the World in Seven Cheap Things: A Guide to Capitalism, Nature, and the Future of the Planet*, Berkeley: University of California Press.

Peck, Jamie (2010), "Zombie Neoliberalism and the Ambidextrous State," *Theoretical Criminology*, 14(1), 104–10.

Pine, B. Joseph and James H. Gilmore (2011), *The Experience Economy*, Harvard Business Press.

Procter, J. (2004), *Stuart Hall*, London: Routledge.

Rabinow, Paul and Nikolas Rose (2003), "Foucault Today," in *The Essential Foucault: Selections from the Essential Works of Foucault, 1954–1984*, New York: New Press, vii–xxv.

Ritzer, George (1996), *The McDonaldization of Society*, Thousand Oaks, CA: Pine Forge Press.

Robinson, William I. (2004), *A Theory of Global Capitalism: Production, Class, and State in a Transnational World*, Baltimore: The John Hokins Uniersity Press.

Rodríguez-Pose, Andrés (2018), "The Revenge of the Places That Don't Matter (and What to Do about It)," *Cambridge Journal of Regions, Economy and Society*, 11(1), 189–209.

Rose, Nikolas (2004), *Powers of Freedom: Reframing Political Thought*, Second, Cambridge: Cambridge University Press.

Runciman, David (2016), "A Win for 'Proper People'?: Brexit as a Rejection of the Networked World," *Juncture*, 23(1), 4–7.

Saatcioglu, Bige and Julie L. Ozanne (2013), "Moral Habitus and Status Negotiation in a Marginalized Working-Class Neighborhood," *Journal of Consumer Research*, 40(4), 692–710.

Scaraboto, Daiane and Eileen Fischer (2013), "Frustrated Fatshionistas: An Institutional Theory Perspective on Consumer Quests for Greater Choice in Mainstream Markets," *Journal of Consumer Research*, 39(6), 1234–57.

Sharifonnasabi, Zahra, Fleura Bardhi, and Marius K. Luedicke (2019), "How Globalization Affects Consumers: Insights from 30 Years of CCT Globalization Research," *Marketing Theory, Online First*. doi: 10.1177/1470593119887469.

Shore, Cris and Susan Wright (2015), "Governing by Numbers: Audit Culture, Rankings and the New World Order: GOVERNING BY NUMBERS," *Social Anthropology*, 23(1), 22–28.

Slater, Don and Fran Tonkiss (2001), *Market Society: Markets and Modern Social Theory*, Cambridge: Polity Press.

Smith, Adam (1937), *The Wealth of Nations*, New York: Random House.

Streeck, Wolfgang (2017), *How Will Capitalism End? Essays on a Failing System*, London: Verso.

Strizhakova, Yuliya, Robin A. Coulter, and Linda L. Price (2008), "Branded Products as a Passport to Global Citizenship: Perspectives from Developed and Developing Countries," *Journal of International Marketing*, 16(4), 57–85.

Taussig, Michael (1991), "Tactility and Distraction," *Cultural Anthropology*, 6(2), 147–53.

Thompson, Craig J. and Zeynep Arsel (2004), "The Starbucks Brandscape and Consumers' (Anticorporate) Experiences of Glocalization," *Journal of Consumer Research*, 31(3), 631–42.

Urry, John (2003), *Global Complexity*, Cambridge: Polity.

Varman, Rohit and Russell W. Belk (2009), "Nationalism and Ideology in an Anticonsumption Movement," *Journal of Consumer Research*, 36(4), 686–700.

Wigger, Angela and Hubert Buch-Hansen (2013), "Competition, the Global Crisis, and Alternatives to Neoliberal Capitalism: A Critical Engagement with Anarchism," *New Political Science*, 35(4), 604–26.

Williamson, J. (1978), *Decoding Advertisements: Ideology and Meaning in Advertising*, London: Marion Boyers.

3

SPORT

Winners, losers, and the logic of competition

Introduction

One of the most resonant images of the London 2012 Olympics was not Michael Phelps becoming the most decorated Olympian of all time, nor was it British athlete Mo Farah crossing the line first in the men's 10,000-m race despite the latter's cultural and national significance, since the sight of a long-distance runner named Mohammad, born in Somaliland, raised in Djibouti, racing in the British colours chimed with the opening ceremony's performance of British 'multicultural nationalism' (Lee and Yoon 2017).

Instead, the creation of McDonald's two-storey pop-up restaurant in the Olympic Park lingers in the collective memory. The story of McDonald's pop-up restaurant made the headlines due to the food giant signing an exclusivity deal meaning other competing food outlets were unable to sell chips (fries) unless they accompanied fish (Booth 2012). Here, Olympians' sporting achievements were overshadowed by yet another instance of global business bullying and dictating smaller, more local commercial outlets (Holt and Cameron 2010).

Athlete activists used to see the Olympic Games as an opportunity to speak to audiences of billions. In 1968, Tommie Smith and John Carlos's Black Power Salutes defined that games, and anti-apartheid demonstrations characterized the 1972 and 1976 Olympics. However, the opportunity to speak to global audiences is now exploited by brands, which seek to use sports as a medium to spread their message. The 'sponsored society' (Holt 2002) has found a welcome home in sport, where all professional sports rely upon some form of sponsorship deal to sustain themselves financially. Moreover, if we consider the way in which nation's governments and cities go out of their way to host the Olympic Games and FIFA's World Cup, it is hard to ignore how sports are for some reason iconic, representative of moral values and ideals that states hold dear (Davies 2012; Holt 2004). While there has been public pushback against hosting the Olympics in recent years, consider British Prime Minister Boris Johnson's promise to bring the World Cup 'home' for 2030 (Smyth 2020), a pledge that will help people forget his previously sport-related incident: him, rugby ball tucked his arm, flooring a 10-year-old boy during a game of touch rugby (Williams 2019).

The aim of this chapter is to explain why sport is held in such high regard by brands, organizations, and governments alike. It is in this historical context that sports marketing and sponsorship has emerged as one of the fastest growing areas of marketing communications (Manoli 2018). Our argument is that sport is deemed particularly valuable in the present because of the way in which sport reinforces a key market logic of our time considered in Chapter 2: competition. To extend these ideas, this chapter contends that sport is held in high political regard because it provides invaluable moral and social justification for the inequalities in outcomes a hyper-competitive, dog-eat-dog society seeks to create and naturalize.

To make this case this chapter proceeds as follows: First, we explore the history, present, and future of sports marketing and explain commonly held views about why sports marketing is successful. Achieving this means we draw on theories of globalization, media, and consumption, and bring these theories to life through examples from English Premier League (EPL) soccer and Indian Premier League (IPL) cricket. Second, we claim that these theories overlook how sport has close and crucial ideological affinities with globalized capitalism and highlight how investment into sports marketing coincides with public denunciations of rampant inequality; we suggest this is no coincidence. Third, we explore this this further and consider how competition helps naturalize competitive dog-eat-dog social behaviours upon which globalized capitalism's growth and expansion depends, as well as how the competitive nature of sport helps render the inequality of outcomes competition engenders morally justifiable and acceptable.

A brief history of sports marketing

Sport and marketing communications haven't always been so entangled, and sporting 'mega-events' (Giulianotti et al. 2014) haven't always been the world's greatest marketing events. The Olympics wasn't always associated with global corporations dictating to smaller firms that they couldn't sell fries. Indeed, in stark contrast to the global sporting spectacle it is today, the Olympics was once a cash-strapped amateur event, where even discussion of commercialization through sponsorship was derided (Smart 2018). For instance, President of the International Olympic Committee, Avery Brundage, declared before the Munich Olympics in 1972 that the games and the governing organizations "should have nothing to do with money" (Barney, Wenn, and Martyn 2002, 100).

This reluctance to consider monetizing the event can be traced back to De Coubertin, founder of the modern Olympics movement, who often spoke of the corrupting influence of money on the amateur spirit and ethos of the game. In 1928, he remained unconvinced that the creation of new stadia had value:

"Almost all the stadiums built in recent are the result of local, and too often, commercial interests, not Olympic interests at all" (De Coubertin 2000, 184). He wasn't just sceptical of the value of new stadia, but turning the Olympics into a commercially based 'mega-event' (Giulianotti et al. 2014), since it would violate and corrupt the game's amateur roots and ethos, explaining that "these oversized showcases are the source of the corruption at the root of … evil" (ibid., 184). It was only during Juan-Antonio Samaranch's premiership in the 1980s that the Olympics abandoned its amateur and non-commercial traditions and embraced the prospect of gold and riches that stem from lucrative sponsorship deals.

Los Angeles Olympic Games in 1984 crossed a threshold with respect to sport sponsorship and advertising. As Alan Tomlinson (2005, 181) puts it, "In LA 1985 everything was for sale". Dubbed the Reagan games, the opening and closing ceremonies were deeply ideological, and looked to advance the superiority of "Western, capitalist, free-American way over the oppressive Eastern, Communist, totalitarian Soviet way" (Lee and Yoon 2017, 956). Both ceremonies sought to stress how it was only the West that promised freedom of expression, unrestrained access to aesthetic and hedonic pleasures, and the virtue of rebellion (Duncan 1986). On American television screens, Budweiser piggybacked off Reagan's call for the blue-collar workers of America to rebuild the nation by thanking those men erecting the nation's infrastructure and coaching American athletes to future success (Holt 2004), paying to use the Olympic five-ring symbol (Barney et al. 2002). On the track, communications giant AT&T paid $11 million to sponsor the torch relay (Tomlinson 2005). The Los Angeles 1984 Olympic Games provided the blueprint for commercialization, with other sports around the world soon following suit.

Italia '90 is arguably the most significant iteration of FIFA's World Cup. It brought football to new UK audiences and did much to dispel the sport's association with tribalistic and violent masculinity. BBC's coverage of the tournament framed football as 'high culture', using Pavarotti's singing of 'Nessan Dorma' as its operatic theme tune, set to the visuals of an opera stage and ballet-like figures dancing around a football (King 2002). Indeed, Williams (2006, 99) explains that "coverage of Italia 90, especially for British television viewers, offered a seductive *bricolage* of theatrical Pavarotti vistas and arias, images of unimagined – at that time – space-age Italian football stadia, and also lovingly framed shots of honed, athletic sporting bodies". Italia '90 therefore set the benchmark for how sport is presented across media. Instead of simply showing the matches live, coverage of Italia '90 focused on telling stories that helped spectators connect to, resonate with, and care about the teams and participations competing (Dunning 1999). It paved the way for football no longer simply being about one team beating another, but about storylines, personalities, and culture. These innovations in the television 'package' turned football into light entertainment, a source of frothy pop culture and 'water-cooler work banter', ultimately a model for how to transform sport into a television spectacle able to generate an audience capable of fetching eye-opening marketing and sponsorship opportunities (Manoli 2018). It therefore set out the blueprint for the Premier League's future global dominance and success (King 2002; Millward 2011).

If the mid-1990s saw the rapid rise of sport sponsorship (McDaniel 1999), the 2010s saw sport sponsorship reach new heights. Those sport brands that exploited latent demand for sponsorship profited the most. Manchester United have an official 'Noodle Partner' and an 'Official Diesel Engine Partner', while Everton are proud of their partnership with snack-sized salami manufacturers (Adamson and Bloor 2014). While this may be the source of criticism, parody, and whimsy, sourcing revenue through sponsorship provides sports clubs with another invaluable stream of revenue to extend that which they receive through broadcasting rights. Indeed, sport's status and economic value are now completely different, with sports marketing and sponsorship currently a mainstream marketing communications tool (Cornwall, Weeks, and Roy 2005), but why?

Why sports marketing?

Sports marketing and sponsorship's growth needs to be understood as an outcome of sports' popularity. The increased status of sport as a tool for marketing communications has been typically understood within theories of globalization, media, and consumption. We review some of these explanations and argue that although each has some merit, they nevertheless overlook the way in which sports create, communicate, and disseminate mythic narratives that help to naturalize and justify the competitive dynamics, practices, and politics associated with globalized capitalism.

Globalization. Globalization recasts sport as an entertainment industry that can be accessed by international audiences. Once regional or national sports now have the capacity to be 'deterritorialized' (see Canniford and Bajde 2015; Preece, Kerrigan, and O'Reilly 2019; Roffe 2020; Sharifonnasabi, Bardhi, and Luedicke 2019) as a result of improvements in picture and sound quality and increased television and satellite coverage. Robinson and Clegg (2018) explain how the EPL gained their market leading position by funnelling early investment into refining the picture and sound quality. As a result, carefully placed microphones pick up and amplify the EPL's distinctive 'soundscape' (Patterson and Larsen 2019). This soundscape isn't like The National Football League (NFL) or rugby in which what officials and referees say is broadcast. No, the EPL's soundscape consists of elderly women questioning the referee's parentage (Hill 2016), lewd chants, and fans' noble attempts to create elaborate songs that use some obscure 70s pop songs as a melody.

The EPL also benefits from its geographical location. Matches kicking off in the early afternoon can be watched by Singaporeans in neighbourhood bars and by New Yorkers as they tuck into their breakfast. As a result, the EPL boast of being broadcast within 212 territories and 725 million homes each weekend. Such figures do not account for the many people who watch the league through 'unofficial' broadcasts (David and Millward 2012).

This one parochial sport where the threat of violence between rival fans hung in the air, along with, as Robinson and Clegg (2018) add, "the smell of urine", has morphed into one where consumers in Mumbai and Johannesburg replicate and amend songs and chants they hear through television broadcasts in EPL's 'official fan parks'. The global diffusion of granular aspects of brand community knowledge (Healy and McDonagh 2013; Pongsakornrungsilp and Schroeder 2011; Schau, Muñiz, and Arnould 2009) means that Ghana Lions, a passionate supporter group of Aston Villa 5,000 miles away from the Birmingham football club's roots, can declare that "There is a god in football and his name is Paul McGrath", a club icon of the late 1980s and the early 1990s (Ampofo 2020). And as in England, passionate rival supporters can turn on each other. In Nairobi's dusty roadside bars, fights can break out between rival supporters who gamble, heckle, and goad one another as live matches are broadcast (BBC 2014). Sports therefore harbour the potential to command the attention of millions. From this globalization perspective, sports marketing's popularity stems from its ability to reach audiences around the world simultaneously.

Spectacular entertainment. In order to better reach and resonate with these global audiences, sports have been reconfigured in the image of spectacular entertainment. Sociologists point to how both the IPL and the EPL have been crafted as contemporary spectacles (Debord 1967), a market-oriented controlled entertainment crafted for the gazing and detached spectator (Giulianotti 2002). Consumer research has previously explained spectacles as staged and dramatized representations of reality (Bradford and Sherry 2015). They are dominant "ideology materialized" (Gilman-Opalsky 2011, 70) in which the interests and values of the powerful are reflected and reinforced. Themed brand stores (Borghini et al. 2009; Kozinets et al. 2002, 2004), tourist locations such as Las Vegas (Belk 2000), and other live sporting events (Bradford and Sherry 2015) are similar commercial contexts in which stupefying awe is conjured. In spectacles, there is little room for consumer transgression, critical involvement, and active participation and, as such, reinforces dominant social structures.

No more is this more pronounced than in IPL cricket. Bear in mind that cricket is a strange sport, as Bill Bryson (2001) explains the sartorial element of the game:

> is an odd game. It is the only sport that incorporates meal breaks. It is the only sport that shares its name with an insect. It is the only sport in which spectators burn as many calories as players -- more if they are moderately restless. It is the only competitive activity of any type, other than perhaps baking, in which you can dress in white from head to toe and be as clean at the end of the day as you were at the beginning.

For those not familiar with it, cricket is a sport that most resembles baseball. There are two teams; each gets the opportunity to accrue 'runs' twice in a game. In contrast to baseball, the bowler pitches the ball after an extended run-up towards the batsman, whose equipment – as intimated by Bryson – makes them look ridiculous. The aim for the batsman is to gain as many runs as possible while not getting 'bowled'. This means there is no necessity for the batsman to hit the ball. There can be spells of the game where the batsman decides to leave the ball for an extended period. However, if he does hit the ball and the ball is caught by an opponent, he can be removed from the game by players in positions that include 'silly point', 'square leg', 'gully', 'fine leg', and 'cow corner'. The traditional version of the game can last five days, and it is possible that there is no winner at the end of it.

This traditional version of cricket bears little resemblance to the most popular and most commercially lucrative version of the sport. The IPL is the most commercialized, glitzy format of cricket. It replaces matches that last five days with ones that end in three hours, substitutes 'sandwiches at tea' for gyrating cheerleaders, and swaps cricket whites for florescent kits. This format removes any incentive for the batsman to leave, or not hit, the ball. Each ball bowled is there to be walloped over the boundary for six runs. It is a bastardized version of the 'gentlemanly' sport 'introduced' through British colonialism (Khondker and Robertson 2018), and it is, for many, all the better for it. In short, the IPL is a quintessential spectacle: "fun-packed entertainment for their children-of-all-ages mass audiences" (Holbrook 2001, 142). Further confirming that the spectacle involves "all that was once directly lived … become[s] mere representation" (Debord 1967, 1), the EPL and IPL's popularity hinges on the exoticization of the locations in which their sports are played.

Exoticization. Exoticization involves representations of the 'other' that create, distort, and stabilize stereotypical and damaging markers of identity (Borgerson and Schroeder 2002). These representations typically reflect existing, obdurate, and historically embedded social hierarchies and binaries – white/black, normal/exotic, rural/urban, and so on. As a result, exoticization acts to amplify and reinforce differences and stereotypes in manners that come to be seen as 'real' (Hall 1997). Globalized capitalism enables exoticization by virtue of how it fuels consumer desire for 'authentic otherness' (Robertson 1992), a desire satiated through 'at hand' or 'at far' encounters with the 'exotic'.

The EPL exoticizes English regional differences to global audiences. 'Northern' clubs such as Burnley and Huddersfield Town are presented as traditionalist, parochial, stuck in their traditions. These clubs are treated as wedded to the past and alien to the frictionless cosmopolitan values of some London clubs such as Arsenal. When Huddersfield Town were promoted to the EPL in 2017, American broadcasters National Broadcasting Company (NBC) introduced their viewers to this Yorkshire city that is known for its links to the industrial revolution and being the origin of rugby league. Club icon Andy Booth explains with his thick Yorkshire accent that "if you come to this town, you better accept our way of life". David Wagner, then Huddersfield manager, is invited to reflect on the differences between the place of his upbringing, Frankfurt, a German city that forms a nodal point in the global financial system that is indifferent to local differences and knowledge, and Huddersfield, a city that, as the presenter reminds him, is 'clearly different', a place untouched by regeneration and modernization, a town like many others in the United Kingdom that "doesn't really matter" (Rodríguez-Pose 2018), neglected by industrial growth strategies and substantial resources, and exists on the margins of today's networked cities and towns (Castells 2009; Runciman 2016).

The EPL is explicit in how it seeks to present clubs to the world by drawing on and accentuate stereotypical depictions of elements of English social life. Ex-CEO of the EPL, Richard Scudamore explained that "In a global world, people have access to just about everything. ... The more global you get, the more local you need to be" (Ebner 2013). Indeed, Robinson explains that the success of the EPL in America can be explained as a result of the "latent Anglophilia ... the images people love when they come over to England for EPL matches are walking narrow streets, smelling burgers, listening to songs, and feeling like there's a fight in the air. They want authenticity" (Cooney 2019). As much as notions of exoticization highlight how sport provides access to 'otherness', it is undeniable that sport also provides rare and unique opportunities to experience oneself as something other than a passive consumer, a theme that has been developed most acutely by sociologists of sport.

Citizenship through consumerism. Because of this aggressive and explicit attempt to transform live sport into a spectacle, one might expect little opportunities for consumers to engage in activity that challenges social mores and political structures (Bradford and Sherry 2015). Yet sociologists explain a fourth reason for sports' growth is that it enables meaningful civic, economic, and political involvement.

It is first a mistake to consider sport fans as simply passive consumers. Fans of EPL are 'working consumers' (Cova and Dalli 2009; Zwick, Bonsu, and Darmody 2008) whose displays of passion and emotion provide the intense and dynamic atmosphere that helps create the television spectacle (Edensor 2015; Hill 2016). Although Andrews and Ritzer (2018) suggest that fan culture is watered down, sanitized, and predictable because of the way in which clubs have introduced a range of cues to elicit singing and chanting, it is incorrect to suggest that the EPL 'fan experience' can be treated as having succumbed to the McDonaldized world of sport, characterized by over the top announcers, blaring music, jumbotrons, and kiss cams.

EPL fan culture is still led by those who do not look to simply take in the match but shape it, transforming themselves into an impassioned crowd. These 'carnival' (Pearson 2012) fans buy into a subculture that contains its own values, rules, and codes. They frown down upon those adults who purchase official club merchandise. They are also naturally dismissive of club attempts to create atmosphere and defy club attempts to manage them. Fans' rebellious character means that the very same fans were at the centre of effective protest against the EPL over ticket prices between 2015 and 2018 (Hill, Canniford, and Millward 2018). Beyond the football fan example, however, there are clearer and more common examples of sports providing a context through which consumers experience themselves as productive political, economic, and social actors.

"Sports chatter" (Whannel 2009) across radio, television, and social media is the grist to the sports entertainment industry mill. The diffusion of social media, coupled with organizational strategies that seek to create consumer involvement in the firm's operations (Canniford 2011; Cova and Dalli 2009; Zwick et al. 2008), means that sport fans produce and consume user-generated content that fuels the media ecosystem (Andrews and Ritzer 2018). The tribal nature of fandom creates alternative and more authentic interpretations of sport events typically offered by mainstream media broadcasters (Norman 2017). Indeed, ArsenalFanTV is a YouTube channel whose primary audience is Arsenal supporters, whose videos find audiences outside of the club's dedicated fan base due to the fans' raw anger, pain, and emotional performances caused by their club's recent fortune and mismanagement (Rivers and Ross 2019). The rise of these 'authentic' media platforms, in conjunction with the blurring of boundaries between 'new' and 'old' media, means that fan-based alternative interpretations of events find their way onto traditional media platforms (Andrews and Ritzer 2018; Jenkins 2008). As a result, there are latent entrepreneurial opportunities for fans to turn themselves into micro-celebrities (Canniford 2011; Cova, Kozinets, and Shankar 2007; Mamali, Nuttall, and Shankar 2018).

All these theories form part of the puzzle to help explain why sports marketing has grown in stature in recent decades. However, we submit that these theories overlook the ideological function of sport in the age of globalized capitalism. What if sport itself embodies an ethos for the continued legitimation of globalized capitalism, capable of naturalizing everyday practices and social events? This function is less to do with locating sports within notions of globalization or media, but instead as having close ideological affinities with globalized capitalism. In the next section, we consider sport as exemplifying the forms of competitive behaviours and social outcomes that globalized capitalism seeks to inculcate, foster, and develop to sustain its existence.

The politics of competition

In contrast to theories of globalization, media and consumption, we argue that sport exemplifies the kinds of activities that globalized capitalism holds dear and wishes to inculcate across economic and social life. Sport, we suggest, serves as an icon of globalized capitalism by virtue of how it embodies and justifies the forms of competitive behaviours and inequality of outcomes and status that globalized capitalism values. We now address each of these points in turn, drawing on marketing communication examples to illustrate how brands and politicians have drawn on these aspects of competition. In so doing, we owe much to Davies (2014, 8) when he claims that "sport has performed a crucial role in cementing certain moral equivalences that are crucial to how neoliberalism works as a political and constitutional project", but would extend this by saying that this doesn't apply to analyses of not only neoliberalism but globalized capitalism.

Competition as a social form

At the heart of political economic thought lies the concept and principle of competition. Adam Smith's (1937) simple statement that markets defining feature is competition over price between sellers and buyers with respect to a specific commodity's supply and demand is no less enduring for its clarity. In other words, price rises correspond to increased competition among buyers for a commodity; conversely, price decreases are caused by increased competition among suppliers. Moreover, competition and its relationship with price provide a formal disciplinary mechanism to motivate suppliers to produce commodities that better meet the changing needs, wants, and desires of consumers (Hayek 2002). It would be a mistake, however, to treat competition as predominantly an economic concept, as to do so misses how competition forms an understanding of society and social relations more generally.

One sociologist who sought to understand competition as it works to shape social relations was Georg Simmel (2008) who, in his 1903 essay, 'The Sociology of Competition', leans heavily on Herbert Spencer's phrase 'the survival of the fittest', a neat summation of Darwin's (1960) revelation that natural selection occurs *within* and *between* species, to conceptualize competition in social life as a form of 'indirect fighting' (Simmel 2008, 961) in which actors seek to attain control over scarce resources, opportunities, and advantages desired by others (Weber 1978; Werron 2015). For Simmel, competition is distinguished from other forms of interaction such as imitation, co-operation, or exchange (Werron 2015). While noting that competitive fields of struggle can be a 'tragedy', for it pits individual against one another, he nevertheless concludes competition in social life is a productive force, since

> the negative entries in the social balance sheet of competition pale beside the incredible synthetic power of the fact that competition in society is competition for human beings, a struggle for applause and attention, for acceptance and devotion of every kind
>
> *(Simmel 2008, 962).*

For Simmel then, competition is a principle around which to organize social life and should be embraced (Gane 2020).

Sport naturalizes dog-eat-dog competitive behaviours

Sport brands have embraced competition as a way to communicate a distinct ideology that speaks to our time. Holt and Cameron (2010, 35), for instance, write of the various ways in which Nike have mobilized an image of the world that is distinctly dystopian: "a Mad–Max world in which broken families, gang-infested housing projects, racist cops, and penitentiary-like schools made life a constant struggle just to sustain a meagre subsistence". This world was brought to life and dramatized by using sportsmen such as Charles Barkley, Tiger Woods, and Michael Jordan to depict their extent of personal sacrifice, determination, and hunger, and their never-say-die attitude that allows them to overcome all obstacles in the pursuit of success.

Though Barkley, Woods, and Jordan found fame in the 1990s, in 2018 Nike released their 'Nothing beats a Londoner' ad, which took much of its inspiration from the success of these advertisements, taking the themes of these adverts and emplacing them in London. Advertising agency Wieden and Kennedy (2018) describe their advert,

> Endlessly enterprising and fiercely competitive, young Londoners shape sport and culture in the metropolis around them. These hungry, resourceful and confident youngsters take us on a whistle-stop tour of their city in Nike's Nothing Beats a Londoner – with the help of cameos from some of the Londoners they look up to – as they strive to one-up each other with their own sporting achievements.

Across all of Nike's adverts, the ultra-competitive aspect of these people's personalities and behaviours is emphasized time and time again. On the one hand, this is a by-product of Nike's distinctive and successful ideology (Holt 2004; Holt and Cameron 2010). On the other hand, it speaks to how sport is the arena of life through which globalized capitalism can help naturalize fiercely competitive and socially destructive 'dog-eat-dog' attitudes and behaviours. This is a Randian world in which people are up against one another, and that any benefits or gains others make come at your own personal expense. This is a world of zero-sum relations, in which winner takes all and losers go home with nothing.

Perhaps it is little surprise that Nike's competitive ideology resonates, for the common thread behind the majority of social policy and welfare reform across advanced capitalist societies including the United Kingdom is that it seeks to place us in a society of constant competition in which we experience others and the rest of society as imposing on our personal freedom (Davies 2014; Gilbert 2019; Srnicek and Williams 2016). As Gilbert (2019, 162) stresses, "we are persistently reminded that our friends and neighbours are in constant competition with us for access to wealth and status". This competitive framing of the world has, to a large extent, been internalized. For Lamont (2019, 666), these competitive "scripts of the self" have been internalized and widely dominant following the global expansion of the 1980s. Indeed, the emphasis on self-reliance can quickly become harmful, since any failure is seen as a personal fault, and receiving help or a 'handout' is viewed as shameful (Gest 2016).

Sport justifies inequalities in outcomes

The second element of sport that helps naturalize competition is that it is used to justify the rampant inequality associated with the post-global financial crisis (GFC) era (Streeck 2017). A dramatic expression of competition's moral and cultural purpose is provided by James Harrison, an American football player who, in 2015, uploaded a picture of two trophies his sons had won. But his message wasn't positive, he wasn't on there to congratulate, nor did he share his pride in their achievements. The caption read:

> While I am very proud of my boys for everything they do and will encourage them till the day I die, these trophies will be given back until they EARN a real trophy. I'm sorry I'm not sorry for believing that everything in life should be earned.

James Harrison had identified the very same frame that 16-year-old William Hague who, when speaking at the Conservative Party Conference in 1977, found a receptive audience when he declared that

> There is at least one school, I think it's in London, where the pupils are allowed to win just one race each, for fear that to win more would make the other pupils seem inferior. That is the illustration of the socialist state.

While they are admittedly strange bedfellows, both James Harrison and William Hague identified how sport's moral and social point is to produce clear winners and losers. Undoubtedly the appeal of sport comes from the inequality of outcomes that result and the drama created in the process. Abandoning the competitive point of sport is therefore not only contradictory but utter lunacy. To paraphrase Hayek (2002), "would we like to know the winner of a football match in advance?" Moreover, it is a moral problem for losers to somehow escape shame and embarrassment. Why, as Hague and Harrison identified, should failure be rewarded?

It is for this reason that sport is used as a rhetorical device by politicians who wish to ignore and justify rank social and economic inequality. In the United Kingdom, there is continued public outrage over bankers' bonuses and 'dodgy' billionaire businessmen, a problem that is a constant thorn in politicians' side (Carruthers and Kim 2011). Sports' power is that it enables politicians to justify and swat away these questions. Indeed, William Davies (2014, 8) goes so far to identify that sport has "performed a crucial role in cementing certain moral equivalences" that underpin the competitive spirit of globalized capitalism, which makes "sport an indispensable symbolic and moral resource". Consider, for instance, how on the run-up to the 2005 UK General Election Jeremy Paxman pressured Tony Blair on the growing levels of inequality the country had seen under his New

Labour government. His answer: "it's not a burning ambition for me to make sure that David Beckham earns less money" (Dorling 2012, 74). It therefore appears that sport is a powerful cultural and moral resource that is capable of explaining away the inequality of outcomes that stem from globalized capitalism.

Sport at a time of political crisis

For some years following the GFC sporting 'mega-events' were a turnoff for country's citizens and politicians. Brazil's FIFA World Cup in 2014 was met by protest (Rosenthal and Cardoso 2015; Saad-Filho 2013), Boston residents mounted a campaign under the name of 'No Boston Olympics' to prevent the games from being held there (Ramaswamy 2015), and residents of the German city of Hamburg voted against hosting the 2024 Olympic and Paralympic Games despite being one of only five cities in contention (BBC 2015). The London 2012 Olympic's legacy is far from perfect, remembered for the fish and chips debate and the bleak, sprawling shopping centre in Stratford, London, it left behind. FIFA's 2022 World Cup in Qatar walks the human rights tight rope and does nothing to commemorate those killed in its construction (Pattison 2019). For a time, it seemed that sport had lost not just its political and cultural purchase but also its romanticism (McDonagh 2017). Sport has however, once again, appeared as an indispensable cultural and moral resource to kick-start a political project.

Boris Johnson, Prime Minister of the United Kingdom, has been urged by his minsters to 'bring football home' by hosting a FIFA World Cup in Manchester in 2030 (Smyth 2020). Given cabinet members of this Conservative government have in the not-so-distant past declared that "the British are among the worst idlers in the world. We work among the lowest hours, we retire early and our productivity is poor. Whereas Indian children aspire to be doctors or businessmen, the British are more interested in football and pop music" (Kwarteng et al. 2012, 61), it is fair to declare sport as a cultural resource able to be used to whip some 'dog-eat-dog', 'chaos capitalism' (O'Toole 2019) spirit into a country shackled by the European Union for too long.

Bibliography

Adamson, Mike and Steven Bloor (2014), "Manchester United's Many Money-Spinning Commercial Deals – in Pictures," *The Guardian*, January 10, https://www.theguardian.com/football/gallery/2013/aug/09/manchester-united-financial-sector.

Ampofo, Owuraku (2020), "The Brilliant Story of Ghana Lions -5,000 Miles Away but Villa All the Way," *birminghammail*, https://www.birminghammail.co.uk/sport/football/football-news/brilliant-story-ghana-lions-5000-17825326.

Andrews, David L. and George Ritzer (2018), "Sport and Prosumption," *Journal of Consumer Culture*, 18(2), 356–73.

Barney, Robert K., Stephen R. Wenn, and Scott G. Martyn (2002), *Selling the Five Rings: The IOC and the Rise of the Olympic Commercialism*, Salt Lake City: The University of Utah Press.

BBC (2014), "Kenyan Fan Stabbed to Death after Arsenal-Liverpool Game," February 10, https://www.bbc.co.uk/news/world-africa-26118063.

———— (2015), "Hamburg Says 'No' to 2024 Olympics," *BBC News*, November 30, https://www.bbc.com/news/world-europe-34960208.Belk, Belk, Russell W. (2000), "May the Farce Be With You: On Las Vegas and Consumer Infantalization," *Consumption, Markets & Culture*, 4(2), 101–24.

Booth, Robert (2012), "Chip-Hungry Olympic Workers Celebrate Freedom from McDonald's Monopoly," *The Guardian*, July 11, https://www.theguardian.com/uk/2012/jul/11/mcdonalds-olympics-chips.

Borgerson, Janet L. and Jonathan E. Schroeder (2002), "Ethical Issues of Global Marketing: Avoiding Bad Faith in Visual Representation," *European Journal of Marketing*, 36(5/6), 570–94.

Borghini, Stefania, Nina Diamond, Robert V. Kozinets, Mary Ann McGrath, Albert M. Muñiz, and John F. Sherry (2009), "Why Are Themed Brandstores So Powerful? Retail Brand Ideology at American Girl Place," *Journal of Retailing*, 85(3), 363–75.

Bradford, Tonya Williams and John F. Sherry (2015), "Domesticating Public Space through Ritual: Tailgating as Vestaval," *Journal of Consumer Research*, 42(1), 130–51.

Bryson, Bill (2001), *In a Sunburned Country*. London: Broadway Books.

Canniford, Robin (2011), "How to Manage Consumer Tribes," *Journal of Strategic Marketing*, 19(5), 453–68.

Canniford, Robin and Domen Bajde, eds. (2015), *Assembling Consumption: Researching Actors, Networks and Markets*, London: Routledge.

Carruthers, Bruce G. and Jeong-Chul Kim (2011), "The Sociology of Finance," *Annual Review of Sociology*, 37(1), 239–59.

Castells, Manuel (2009), *The Rise of the Network Society*, 1, Second Edition, Oxford: Blackwell.

Cooney, Gavin (2019), "How the Premier League Became 'Britain's Most Successful Export since The Beatles,' " *The42*, https://www.the42.ie/the-club-book-4434028-Jan2019/.

Cornwall, T. Bettina, Clinton S. Weeks, and Donald P. Roy (2005), "Sponsorship-Linked Marketing: Opening the Black Box," *Journal of Advertising*, 34(2), 21–42.

Cova, Bernard and Daniele Dalli (2009), "Working Consumers: The Next Step in Marketing Theory?," *Marketing Theory*, 9(3), 315–39.

Cova, Bernard, Robert V. Kozinets, and Avi Shankar, eds. (2007), *Tribes, Inc.*, Oxford: Elsevier.

Darwin, Charles (1960), *The Origin of the Species*, New York: Mentor.

David, Matthew and Peter Millward (2012), "Football's Coming Home?: Digital Reterritorialization, Contradictions in the Transnational Coverage of Sport and the Sociology of Alternative Football Broadcasts: Football's Coming Home?," *The British Journal of Sociology*, 63(2), 349–69.

———— (2012), "The Promises of Sport," https://www.academia.edu/5236439/THE_PROMISES_OF_SPORT.

Davies, William (2014), *The Limits of Neoliberalism: Authority, Sovereignty and the Logic of Competition*, London: SAGE.De Coubertin, Pierre (2000), *Pierre de Coubertin 1863–1937: Olympism, Selected Writing*, ed. Norbert Muller, Lausanne: International Olympic Committee.

Debord, Guy (1967), *The Society of the Spectacle*, New York: Zone Books.

Dorling, Daniel (2012), *Fair Play: A Daniel Dorling Reader on Social Justice*, London: Policy Press.

Duncan, Margaret Carlisle (1986), "A Hermeneutic of Spectator Sport: The 1976 and 1984 Olympic Games," *Quest*, 38(1), 50–77.

Dunning, Eric (1999), *Sports Matters: Sociological Studies of Sport, Violence and Civilization*, London: Routledge.

Ebner, S. (2013), "History and Time Are Key to Power of Football, Says Premier League Chief," *The Times*, http://www.thetimes.co.uk/tto/public/ceo-summit/article3804923.ece.

Edensor, Tim (2015), "Producing Atmospheres at the Match: Fan Cultures, Commercialisation and Mood Management in English Football," *Emotion, Space and Society*, 15, 82–89.

Gane, Nicholas (2020), "Competition: A Critical History of a Concept," *Theory, Culture & Society*, 37(2), 31–59.

Gest, J. (2016), *The New Minority: White Working Class Politics in an Age of Immigration and Inequality*, Oxford: Oxford University Press.

Gilbert, Jeremy (2019), "The Joy of Co-production," *IPPR Progressive Review*, 26(2), 161–72.

Gilman-Opalsky, Richard (2011), *Spectacular Capitalism: Guy Debord and the Practice of Radical Philosophy*, New York: Autonomedia.

Giulianotti, Richard (2002), "Supporters, Followers, Fans, and Flaneurs: A Taxonomy of Spectator Identities in Football," *Journal of Sport and Social Issues*, 26(1), 25–46.

Giulianotti, Richard, Gary Armstrong, Gavin Hales, and Dick Hobbs (2014), "Global Sport Mega-Events and the Politics of Mobility: The Case of the London 2012 Olympics: Global Sport Mega-Events and the Politics of Mobility," *British Journal of Sociology*, 66(1), 118–40.

Hall, Stuart (1997), *Representation: Cultural Representations and Signifying Practices*, London: SAGE.

Hayek, F. A. (2002), "Competition as a Discovery Procedure," *The Quarterly Journal of Austrian Economics*, 5(3), 9–23.

Healy, Jason C. and Pierre McDonagh (2013), "Consumer Roles in Brand Culture and Value Co-Creation in Virtual Communities," *Journal of Business Research*, 66(9), 1528–40.

Hill, Tim (2016), "Mood-Management in the English Premier League," in *Assembling Consumption: Researching Actors, Networks and Markets*, eds. Robin Canniford and Domen Bajde, London: Routledge, 155–71.

Hill, Tim, Robin Canniford, and Peter Millward (2018), "Against Modern Football: Mobilising Protest Movements in Social Media," *Sociology*, 52(4), 688–708.

Holbrook, M. B. (2001), "Times Square, Disneyphobia, and HegeMickey: The Ricky Principle, and the Downside of the Entertainment Economy – It's Fun-Dumb-Mental," *Marketing Theory*, 1(2), 139–63.

Holt, Douglas B. (2002), "Why Do Brands Cause Trouble? A Dialectical Theory of Consumer Culture and Branding," *Journal of Consumer Research*, 29(1), 70–90.

———— (2004), *How Brands Become Icons: The Principles of Cultural Branding*, London: Harvard Business Press.

Holt, Douglas B. and Douglas Cameron (2010), *Cultural Strategy: Using Innovative Ideologies to Build Breakthrough Brands*, Oxford: Oxford University Press.

Jenkins, H. (2008), *Convergence Culture: Where Old and New Media Collide*, New York: New York Press.

Khondker, Habibul Haque and Roland Robertson (2018), "Glocalization, Consumption, and Cricket: The Indian Premier League," *Journal of Consumer Culture*, 18(2), 279–97.

King, Anthony (2002), *The End of the Terraces: The Transformation of English Football*, Revised edition, Leicester: Leicester University Press.

Kozinets, Robert V., John F. Sherry, Benet DeBerry-Spence, Adam Duhachek, Krittinee Nuttavuthisit, and Diana Storm (2002), "Themed Flagship Brand Stores in the New Millennium: Theory, Practice, Prospects," *Journal of Retailing*, 78(1), 17–29.

Kozinets, Robert V., John F. Sherry, Jr., Diana Storm, Adam Duhachek, Krittinee Nuttavuthisit, and Benét DeBerry-Spence (2004), "Ludic Agency and Retail Spectacle," *Journal of Consumer Research*, 31(3), 658–72.

Kwarteng, Kwasi, Priti Patel, Dominic Raab, Chris Skidmore, and Elizabeth Truss (2012), *Brittania Unchained*, London: Palgrave Macmillan.

Lamont, Michèle (2019), "From 'Having' to 'Being': Self-worth and the Current Crisis of American Society," *The British Journal of Sociology*, 70(3), 660–707.

Lee, Jongsoo and Hyunsun Yoon (2017), "Narratives of the Nation in the Olympic Opening Ceremonies: Comparative Analysis of Beijing 2008 and London 2012: Narratives of the Nation in the Olympic Opening Ceremonies," *Nations and Nationalism*, 23(4), 952–69.

Mamali, Elizabeth, Peter Nuttall, and Avi Shankar (2018), "Formalizing Consumer Tribes: Towards a Theorization of Consumer-Constructed Organizations," *Marketing Theory*, 18(4), 521–42.

Manoli, Argyro Elisavet (2018), "Sport Marketing's Past, Present and Future; an Introduction to the Special Issue on Contemporary Issues in Sports Marketing," *Journal of Strategic Marketing*, 26(1), 1–5.

McDonagh, Pierre (2017), "Football – Marketplace Icon?," *Consumption Markets & Culture*, 20(1), 7–11.

Millward, Peter (2011), *The Global Football League*, London: Palgrave Macmillan, http://link.springer.com/10.1057/9780230348639.

Norman, M. (2017), "Serious Leisure, Prosumption and the Digital Sport Media Economy: A Case Study of Ice Hocking Blogging," in *Digital Leisure Cultures: Critical Perspectives*, eds. S. Canicelli, D. McGillivray, and G. McPherson, Abingdon: Routledge, 80–93.

O'Toole, Fintan (2019), *Heroic Failure: Brexit and the Politics of Pain*, London: Apollo.

Patterson, Maurice and Gretchen Larsen (2019), "Listening to Consumption: Towards a Sonic Turn in Consumer Research," *Marketing Theory*, 19(2), 105–27.

Pearson, Geoff (2012), *An Ethnography of English Football Fans: Cans, Cops, and Carnivals*, Manchester: Manchester Unity Press.

Pongsakornrungsilp, Siwarit and Jonathan E. Schroeder (2011), "Understanding Value Co-Creation in a Co-Consuming Brand Community," *Marketing Theory*, 11(3), 303–24.

Preece, Chloe, Finola Kerrigan, and Daragh O'Reilly (2019), "License to Assemble: Theorizing Brand Longevity," *Journal of Consumer Research*, 46(2), 330–50.

Ramaswamy, Chitra (2015), "Hosting the Olympics: The Competition No One Wants to Win," *The Guardian*, November 30, https://www.theguardian.com/sport/shortcuts/2015/nov/30/hosting-olympics-hamburg-drop-out-2024-games.

Rivers, Damian J. and Andrew S. Ross (2019), "'This Channel Has More Subs from Rival Fans than Arsenal Fans': Arsenal Fan TV, Football Fandom and Banter in the New Media Era," *Sport in Society*, Online First.

Robertson, Roland (1992), *Globalization: Social Theory and Global Culture*, London: Sage.

Robinson, Joshua and Jonathan Clegg (2018), *The Club: How the English Premier League Became the Wildest, Richest, Most Disruptive Force in Sports*, Boston, MA: Houghton Mifflin Harcourt.

Rodríguez-Pose, Andrés (2018), "The Revenge of the Places That Don't Matter (and What to Do about It)," *Cambridge Journal of Regions, Economy and Society*, 11(1), 189–209.

Roffe, Jon (2020), *The Works of Gilles Deleuze I: 1953–1969*, Melbourne: re.press.

Rosenthal, Benjamin and Flavia Cardoso (2015), "'There Will Not Be a World Cup': THe Kratophanous Power of the FIFA 2014 World Cup in Brazil," in *Consumer Culture Theory (Research in Consumer Behavior, Vol. 17)*, London: Emerald Group Publishing Limited, 367–99.

Runciman, David (2016), "A Win for 'Proper People'?: Brexit as a Rejection of the Networked World," *Juncture*, 23(1), 4–7.

Saad-Filho, Alfredo (2013), "Mass Protests under 'Left Neoliberalism': Brazil, June-July 2013," *Critical Sociology*, 39(5), 657–69.

Schau, Hope Jensen, Albert M. Muñiz, and Eric J. Arnould (2009), "How Brand Community Practices Create Value," *Journal of Marketing*, 73(5), 30–51.

Sharifonnasabi, Zahra, Fleura Bardhi, and Marius K. Luedicke (2019), "How Globalization Affects Consumers: Insights from 30 Years of CCT Globalization Research," *Marketing Theory, Online First*.

Simmel, George (2008), "The Sociology of Competition," *Canadian Journal of Sociology*, 33(4), 957–78.

Smart, Barry (2018), "Consuming Olympism: Consumer Culture, Sport Star Sponsorship and the Commercialisation of the Olympics," *Journal of Consumer Culture*, 18(2), 241–60.

Smith, Adam (1937), *The Wealth of Nations*, New York: Random House.

Smyth, Chris (2020), "Ministers Push Boris Johnson for a Manchester World Cup Final," *The Times*, January 1, https://www.thetimes.co.uk/article/ministers-push-boris-johnson-for-a-manchester-world-cup-final-0ppg7bd28.

Srnicek, Nick and Alex Williams (2016), *Inventing the Future: Postcapitalism and a World without Work*, London: Verso.

Streeck, Wolfgang (2017), *How Will Capitalism End? Essays on a Failing System*, London: Verso.

Tomlinson, Alan (2005), "The Commercialization of the Olympics: Cities, Corporations, and the Olympic Commodity," in *The Global Olympics: Historical and Sociological Studies of the Modern Games*, eds. Kevin B. Warmsley and Kevin Mary Young, Amsterdam: Elsevier, 179–200.

Weber, Max (1978), *Economy and Society, Volume One*, Berkeley, CA: University of California Press.

Werron, Tobias (2015), "Why Do We Believe in Competition? A Historical-Sociological View of Competition as an Institutionalized Modern Imaginary," *Distinktion: Journal of Social Theory*, 16(2), 186–210.

Whannel, G. (2009), "Between Culture and Economy: Understanding the Politics of Media Sport," in *Marxism, Cultural Studies and Sport*, eds. B. Carrington and I. McDonald, London: Routledge, 68–87.

Wieden+Kennedy (2018), "Nike – Nothing Beats a Londoner," *W+K London*, /work/nothing-beats-londoner/.

Williams, John (2006), "'Protect Me From What I Want': Football Fandom, Celebrity Cultures and 'New' Football in England," *Soccer & Society*, 7(1), 96–114.

Williams, Richard (2019), "Making Political Capital from Sport Comes Naturally to Boastful Boris Johnson | Richard Williams," *The Guardian*, December 27, https://www.theguardian.com/football/blog/2019/dec/27/political-capital-sport-boris-johnson-world-cup-2030-football.

Zwick, Detlev, Samuel K. Bonsu, and Aron Darmody (2008), "Putting Consumers to Work: Co-Creation and New Marketing Govern-Mentality," *Journal of Consumer Culture*, 8(2), 163–96.

4

CORPORATE SOCIAL RESPONSIBILITY

Corporate utopias, wishful thinking, and the logic of sustainability

Introduction

One of the defining features of capitalism is its remarkable ability to endure. Its champions proclaim that it is the epitome of social and economic progress, that there is no alternative to it, and that those who prosper in it do so because of their willpower, and 'can do' attitude, rather than any other predisposed advantages. Indeed, it is an oft heard truism that "when the going gets tough, the tough get going". In this chapter, we focus on how organizations tell sophisticated stories (Gabriel 2000; Woodside et al. 2008) that express how well things are going, that everything is fine, that there is nothing to worry about, and that everything is under control. We write this while Australia's wildlife dies and nature burns (Karp 2019), Europe is wrecked by storms, and politicians refuse to speak about or deny the climate emergency (Galvin 2020). There is little to no response, as they drag their heels to act.

This chapter concerns sustainability and the way in which organizations, brands, and politicians have sought to renew people's trust in globalized capitalism's ability to provide an ecologically sustainable future for everyone. In it, we first assess the extent of corporate social responsibility's (CSR) growth within management and marketing studies. We then suggest that CSR needs to be considered a form of marketing communications that seeks to restore trust and legitimacy in business in the face of ecological breakdown. In doing so, we extend the critique of CSR that treats "perfect information is the economic myth: disingenuous persuasion is the 'murketing' reality" (Dunne 2018, 1310).

Sustainability: profit and/or people?

To begin, however, a pedantic point. Sustainability is often used in different ways by various people. It is a true buzz word of contemporary after all. Economists will typically use the term to refer to the ability to endure, or last. For example, organizations and their business models will be discussed in terms of their viability to create and sustain jobs for workers and generate surplus value in the production process. It is therefore important, from the outset, that this as economic sustainability is compared to the alternative usage, which concerns ecological sustainability. In contrast, this refers to the planetary carrying capacity for humanity, and how organizations and society impact on this.

Business and organizations now use sustainability in both of these ways, as not only do they argue for a continuance of the ways they conduct business – in terms of their lasting viability – but they also map out plans they have to develop their vision of ecological sustainability and how they contribute, rather than detract, to humanity's life on this planet. Consider, for instance, Sustainable Life Media's Sustainable Brands initiative, which encapsulates both elements of sustainability. It is the best of utopian thinking, a place where a self-proclaimed premier community of brand innovators and bright thinkers shape the future of commerce worldwide, simultaneously saving the planet while making some profit. Consider the way Sustainable Life Media (2019) describes its purpose, belief, and ethos,

> Since 2006, our goal has been to inspire, engage, and equip business leaders and practitioners who see social and environmental challenges as an essential driver of brand innovation, value creation, and positive impact. We Believe: Brands are uniquely positioned to align business and society on the path to a flourishing future. Those brands that embrace this challenge will prosper in the 21st century. Accomplishing this challenge requires a new way of seeing the world - along with a new set of skills, tools, and collaborators.

In this regard, there is a sense that the corporation is indeed now very much helping to shape this discourse and is patterning the public's understanding of what needs to be done with visions of corporate sustainability. These visions depict corporations as ever-willing and useful *solution providers*, supplying answers to the social, environmental, and ecological ills and hazards of society (see McDonagh et al. 2014). There is, of course, little recognition or reflection on the fact that many of the same organizations have historically been culpable in creating alarming social, environmental, and ecological damage. In much of the same way that 'Big Tech' wants to solve the problems of fake news, conspiracy theory, and other related democratic dangers in exchange for our data, business and organizations want us to exchange cash for their products and services while they provide solutions to our ecological problems (Olah 2019).

How did we get to this point?

In the early 1990s, McDonagh (1995, 1998) argued for the pressing need to develop a theory of sustainable communication in order to help people understand the present and future ecological consequences of a capitalism that saw no limits to the land and labour it could plunder. In doing so, the process of sustainable communication was described as an interactive social process of unravelling and eradicating ecological alienation that occurs between an organization and its publics or stakeholders (see also McDonagh 2002). Put simply, how would anyone standing outside a factory in a local community know if it was doing good or bad things ecologically speaking?

Its focal point was ecological sustainability, not social responsiveness, and it called for greater access to organizations and increased transparency of operations and the labour process. It also stressed the importance of geo-indicators as markers of progress and the purposeful engagement of critics and concerned publics by organizations. In many ways, this utopian or naïve call for businesses to make clear its ecological credentials marked the cards of marketers within corporations to expect even greater scrutiny about their ecological consequences than had happened in the past. Even in the early 1990s, this type of process was deemed to represent both an auditing challenge that was formidable and quite a resource heavy implication if the operations of a firm were to be laid bare for those wishing to scrutinize activities from an ecological point of view. In other words, which people within an organization would be charged and resourced with the task to collate appropriate ecological data to assess the situation and then be employed to deal with external or internal queries on these matters. At the time McDonagh detailed significant organizational, social, and marketing barriers that needed to be surmounted before sustainable communication might actually come into play. Such obstacles, Kilbourne (2004) agreed, were unlikely to alter due to society's institutions fixation over the past 300 year's economic progress (Kilbourne 2009; McDonagh, Kilbourne, and Prothero 2014).

Since then, however, Castells' (2009a, 2009b) tentative techno-utopian prediction, that information will be more readily accessed as part and parcel of the development of the network society, has enabled people to retrieve information about organizations. While such ease of access to information has been enabled some degree of critical scrutiny, the full potential of sustainable communication is yet to be fully realized. Indeed, the development of new forms of communication has intensified and accelerated the manner in which organizations communicate to their audience and world at large. Marketing communications has thus been extended to help organizations in this respect. It would now seem that not since the creation of the Scarlet Pimpernel[1] has there been such a need to rescue the aristocracy of corporations from the slings and arrows of the latest calls for transparency.

Corporate social responsibility

Within this context it seems that there is great sympathy for the Dragons of CSR which many researchers in management believe can save the day. While there has been a flurry of scholarship in the field of CSR, it still represents significant theoretical challenges (Dunne 2008). For the purposes of our analysis, in this text it would appear CSR has become the most recent addition to what marketers traditionally call the tools of marketing communications or corporate marketing. By way of simple reminder as to why we make this claim consider how marketing communications is defined as follows by Keller (2009, 139) as,

> the means by which firms attempt to inform, persuade and remind consumers – directly or indirectly – about the products and brands they sell. In a sense, marketing communications represent the 'voice' of the company and its brands and are a means by which it can establish a dialogue and build relationships with and among consumers.

Over the course of history, marketing communications typically proffers a rather benign view of how organizations match the needs of customers with organizational products (Tadajewski and Brownlie 2009) or services under the increasingly heady and popular mantra of service-dominant logic (see Hietanen, Andéhn, and Bradshaw 2018), "that's customer service at all costs mam", or as part of the market as a sign system (Firat, Peñaloza, and Venkatesh 2014). It seems that building a good 'reputation' (Brammer and Pavelin 2004) remains the mainstay of much CSR, as much as we can say Shakespeare's *Iago* was a truth talker. In terms of how marketers have developed their thinking on corporate marketing, Balmer and Greyser (2006, 732) observed that

> From the outset we wish to make it clear that corporate marketing has a general applicability to entities whether they are corporations, companies, not-for-profit organisations as well as other categories such as business alliances, cities and so on. A key attribute of corporate-level marketing is its concern with multiple exchange relationships with multiple stakeholder groups and networks. Another feature is the importance accorded to the temporal dimension with there being fidelity not only to present relationships but those of the past and those prospective relationships of the future.

This definition is quite close to the desire to theorize multiple stakeholder groups for an organization that encapsulates a lot of CSR scholarship. It seems odd then that in terms of attempts to define CSR, leading scholars in that area make the following observation: "In the contested world of CSR, it is virtually impossible to provide a definitive answer to the question of what CSR 'really' is" (Crane, Matten, and Spence 2008, 5). This we submit may be simply ascribed to the difficulty of redefining aspects of marketing communications or corporate marketing as new fields of study in and of themselves. We have to note that while much of the past 200 years has been spent prefiguring the problems of modernity (cf Kilbourne 2004, 2009; McDonagh et al. 2014), it has only recently witnessed the deliberations of the management scholars who have mostly rallied about concepts such as CSR as a worthy field of inquiry, as evidenced by the numbers of articles that are appearing on this topic even in these 'lesser' journals (see Table 4.1).

To assess the extent to which CSR has been taken up as a broad rubric through which to understand how business and organizations are rallying behind the CSR cause, at the end of 2018 the authors performed a selected content analysis of papers in several of the Chartered Association of Business Schools (CABS) lesser revered journals. It became evident that a number of articles have focussed on CSR-related challenges.

As one colleague James Fitchett observed in the early 1990s, this emerging fascination with CSR is akin to people playing with mirrors, ropes, and pulleys to distract the public from what organizations are doing with and to the environment. As such, CSR can be classed as a form of marketing communications which clearly has instrumentality at its heart and deserves fuller scrutiny for its role in ideologically propping up globalized capitalism at a time of crisis. We are not alone in suggesting this. Dunne (2008) notes that the one thing 50 years of research into CSR shows us clearly is that the organization requires a moral compass. Following Dunne, it can be argued that it has become popular to argue for the belief in the need for CSR. Of late, writing in the revered *Journal of Management Studies*, Crane and Glozer (2016, 2) observed that CSR communication is an embedded part of what they term 'stakeholder management',

> As corporate responsibilities have increasingly expanded due to heightened stakeholder expectations in a globalized economy…, the way in which organizations communicate with their stakeholders through CSR communication has become a subject of intense scrutiny.

This again seems to build on marketing communications which also has witnessed the steady growth of public relations (PR) as a separate field of study to marketing which has been steadily led by scholars like Jacquie L'Etang (1994, 2005). In the mid-1990s former Tory MP and journalist Matthew Parris narrated

TABLE 4.1 CSR papers in selected journals

Journal	Number
Business & Society	649
Culture and Organisation	109
Journal of Business Ethics	559
Journal of Consumer Culture	5 (including two book reviews)
Journal of Macromarketing	281
Journal of Marketing Management	91

Channel 4's *Without Walls* documentary 'PRism': Bad Ideas of the 20th Century. This programme shows inter alia the use of PR by British Nuclear Fuels Limited (BNFL) to portray nuclear energy as community friendly. Parris shows how BNFL employ cows to graze alongside Sellafield which has had its name changed from Windscale following a prior leak. They also have a science exhibition on-site to showcase the technology of nuclear fusion and educate the public. All this communicates the organization as a benign force of nature. Likewise, Parris submits that PR always 'accentuates the positive' pointing the finger at himself and shows how he gets a PR-advised makeover to appear like the perfect journalist – new suit, haircut, and appropriate briefcase. He underscores in the process how this is all about 'seeming' and nothing to do with substance.

We submit that readers should best equip themselves to think of critical marketing communications as being inclusive of Keller's definition as well as the use of a corporate marketing definition which clearly includes PR, lobbying, and CSR as sophisticated marketing activities that require further scrutiny. In this way, one is better placed to acknowledge and unpack the instrumentality that emanates from an organization's communicative acts. At a time in human history when organizations are being quizzed and called to account on issues as varied as their impact on the environment, their treatment of people of differing genders, pay inequality and labour practices at home or in their supply chain the tired arsenal of traditional marketing communications needed to be reinforced or strengthened. As a consequence, it has expanded into sophisticated messaging that draws on the techniques of lobbying, PR event management, doing good through CSR storytelling and outreach programmes, and celebrating the positive related to the organization through social media platforms.

To view marketing communications critically is an extension of early work by Judith Williamson (1978) that seeks to demonstrate how cultural elements are appropriated by organizations into their selling activities, work which was followed by later work by critical sociologists Goldman and Papson (1994, 1996) who point out how advertising became a dominant global force raiding the referent system of popular culture to appellate consumers. At the turn of the century, Schroeder (2002, 14) argued that branding in which marketing communications is inculcated had truly entered the political sphere. Moreover, others noted that brands were not just a cultural phenomenon but constituted a capitalist institution which created their own productive practices (Arvidsson 2006; Bradshaw, McDonagh, and Marshall 2006; Zwick and Cayla 2011). It is this that the reader needs to be mindful about as such brand culture has employed CSR on behalf of the organization to build the value of the organization and its branding in the eyes of its stakeholders. In one sense, viewing marketing communications critically is akin to the concept of *refusal* as discussed in cultural anthropology; McGranahan (2016, 320) notes it as follows:

> In our research, we collectively find refusals of both formal and everyday relations, including between claimed equals, in ways that redirect levels of

engagement. We see individuals and collectives refusing affiliations, identities, and relationships in ways that are not about domination or class struggle (Scott 1985; Sivaramakrishnan 2005), but instead about staking claims to the sociality that underlies all relationships, including political ones. In that sense, we see refusal as genealogically linked to resistance, but not as one and the same.

What is interesting here in this work is that it suggests the term *refusal* is appropriate as a limit of some sort has been reached, or as McGranahan suggests, it is *a way of shedding light on something we have missed* both as subject and as method. She sees it as being generative, willful, social, and affiliative, and not just another form of resistance. In many respects she sees 'the present' as very much in need of refusal. McGranahan (2016, 323) finishes her introduction by saying of *refusal*,

> the current political moment demands it. As we find our bearings in the present, it is clear the social and political terrains have shifted for many around the world. Occupy. Black Lives Matter. Idle No More. The Umbrella Movement. The Sunflower Student Movement. 360.org. Decolonizing the Academy. The list could go on and on. The list does go on and on. If refusal is continually appearing in the present moment as creative and potent, then our job is to consider how and why. We invite you to join us in the work of thinking through refusal as ethnographic concept and practice.

To begin to refuse then is to view things more critically. We note that Hackley (2019, 189) hints at part of some of this transmogrification when he issues a clarion call to critical researchers to focus more time considering the *process* of advertising production rather than just the advertisements themselves:

> What advertisements look like is changing. Marketing communication disciplines that, since the 1960s, involved different career paths in different cultural industries, such as Public Relations, script writing, copywriting, animation, digital and art production, not to mention consumer and market research and brand planning, are now often deployed under the same roof in all-purpose marketing and media content agencies that produce multichannel promotional campaigns. The practices of advertising production are changing as the media landscape for advertising changes. This renders critical analyses of advertising practices from the production side complex and problematic. Nonetheless, the processes of advertising production remain a key site with which critical marketing researchers need to engage.

To practice critical marketing communications requires an evidence-based form of inquiry, which permits claims made by organizations to be cross-checked and verified (McDonagh and Prothero 2015; Mullen 2010) so that we do not have cases of deception or misleading communications circulating in the market place. In this regard, we submit that it is time to have reached 'our limit' of missing such deception.

Dark (murky) waters

There are clear instances of CSR-focussed marketing communications misleading the lay person. Consider how Dupont presently describes its efforts at sustainability,

> Today, we continue that tradition at the new DuPont with a renewed sense of urgency for the times in which we live. Through our science, our people and our communities, we pledge to constantly improve and innovate more sustainable ways of contributing. This is our commitment to our shared humanity and to helping every community thrive for generations to come. It's time for generation n:ow.
>
> *(available online at https://www.dupont.com/about/sustainability.html*
> *accessed 02 Feb 2020)*

As this book goes to press, the Dupont corporation is the focal point for a box office movie *Dark Waters* which problematizes how the people in Dupont hid the adverse health consequences of PFOA-C8 which, after a legal lawsuit filed in 2001, was proven in 2017 (16 years later) to cause kidney and testicular cancer, ulcerative colitis, thyroid disease, pregnancy-induced hypertension, and high cholesterol (Reuters 2017). Dupont, a multi-billion-dollar corporation, eventually settled about 3,550 cases for around US$671 million, which is less than one year's profit from the Teflon range of products alone. Furthermore, one aspect of education displays all the hallmarks of murky waters at play as the myth of the 'real world' persists in the common vernacular. Apparently, there is a 'real-world learning outcome' through the inculcation of students in industry challenges around, say, sustainability. It is debatable if the language of 'real-world' versus otherworld actually makes any sense in 2020, but most readers will no doubt have had a least one colleague who makes the distinction in daily conversations over coffee.

Consider too how Johnson & Johnson describes its work towards sustainability, as you are confronted by a range of Johnson & Johnson stories and also a note of its heritage; one such story is entitled 'The X Factor: How Johnson & Johnson Has Helped Ignite the Power of Women Since 1886' (see https://www.jnj.com/our-heritage/how-johnson-johnson-has-supported-womens-empowerment-since-1886).

This public relating is not surprising given we are in 2020 and presently there are talcum powder lawsuits being filed by some 15,500 women in relation to ovarian cancer. Indeed, evidence demonstrates that Johnson & Johnson knew that their talcum powder contained cancer-causing asbestos, which is leading to repeated talcum powder lawsuit verdicts in favour of plaintiffs (Meneo 2020) while at the same time the Chief Executive Officer (CEO) claims that the product is safe to use (Loftus 2020).

One of the authors has first-hand experience of having worked, in the recent past, in murky water with an industrially focussed big pharma collaborative. This was to organize an educational event for postgraduate business students in both Ireland and the United States to see what big business was doing regarding sustainability. The event was sponsored by Johnson & Johnson as part of its sustainability outreach efforts alongside some of its suppliers and educational partners. During the initial seminar organization process, it was clear to the author that corporate PR was at play, and indeed the resultant press coverage confirmed as much (Devereux 2012; the Sustainable SME):

> I arrived into our dinner meeting before departing for NJ corporate headquarters in the morning. I was ready to tell him exactly what value I placed on this new term. I was introduced but wasn't expecting this guy to be so disarmingly charismatic. A diversity scholar, naturally, double-purple hearts for service in VN and to boot a genuine family guy. I'm the *fall guy* (emphasis added) here. I smiled, then said 'Hello there, let's talk sustainability, shall we?
>
> *(SustaiNext EU Field Notes, New York, November 4th 2011).*

Such PR events will continue to grow as industry–university liaison gathers apace. In this context and who can argue against the ethos of closer observation of what industry is up to. Many of our students will enter into lifetime contractual employment with these corporations, and we as academics have a responsibility to both sides to make sure they understand the 'rules of the game' at play in this market.

Jacqui L'Étang (2015) talks of the difficulty of understanding critical PR as anything other than a position at the margins and of her use of conceptual black humour as 'CPR' is deliberately used in tandem for cardio pulmonary resuscitation. We too find ourselves occupying such a space and trying to re-awaken reflection in students. L'Etang laments, in her introduction to the CPR handbook, colleagues trapped into the delivery of functional degrees while their souls cry out for more critical stances. Indeed, it seems a popular argument which implies that we are not alone with these thoughts. Emma O'Kelly (2019), writing as an education correspondent for Raidió Teilifís Éireann (RTE), remarks on what the President of Ireland, Michael D Higgins, opines,

> The president, Michael D Higgins, has criticised "many universities" who he says now produce graduates who are "professionals" rather than "critically engaged citizens".
>
> In a speech at Fordham University in New York Mr Higgins accused universities of abandoning their "traditional role" of preparing students to be "thoughtful, conscientious, active citizens".
>
> He said instead they aimed "almost exclusively" towards preparing them for the global marketplace.
>
> *Available Online at https://www.rte.ie/news/education/2019/*
> *0930/1079255-michael-d-higgins/ accessed 02 Feb 2020*

The reader should perhaps pause to consider how best to interpret the recent advert by Amazon called 'Work Hard', which obfuscates the labour process in its organization for the lay person. The advert lauds the work environment and has been described as follows (iSpot.TV 2019):

> Amazon Warehouse workers talk about why they love working with the company. One man got full healthcare, vision and dental coverage from the start and it's the first time in his life he's gotten that. Another worker loves that Amazon is a trans-friendly work environment and that their boss is an advocate for them. A third employee is working her way through college and Amazon is helping pay for it. Amazon invites you to apply at its website.

This marketing communication effects a narrative of Amazon being a responsible employer and belies the extensive efforts that Amazon goes to dissuade workers from unionization within the labour process (Fortson 2019; Wolfe-Robinson 2019). The organization Corpwatch (Greenhouse 2000) shows how much effort Amazon goes to prevent workers organizing in a trade union. In a detailed commentary, Greenhouse outlines how Amazon.com threw resources into a campaign to stop new unionization. The company told its workers that unions were a greedy for-profit set-up and that the company favoured organizing and offering managers some insights into how to spot when workers were trying to back a union. On the internal company web page for the company, they provided supervisors with anti-union propaganda to distribute to employees. This material argued that unions would mean strife and claimed that unions were likely to charge members expensive membership fees while not being able to deliver improvements to working wages or employee benefits.

> Among the signs that Amazon notes are "hushed conversations when you approach which have not occurred before," and "small group huddles breaking up in silence on the approach of the supervisor." Other warning signs, according to the site, are an increase in complaints, a decrease in quality of work, growing aggressiveness and dawdling in the lunchroom and restrooms.
>
> Amazon, one of the leaders in retailing and on-demand web-services, has stepped up its anti-union activities last week after two unions and an independent organizing group announced plans to speed efforts to unionize Amazon during the holiday e-shopping rush. The organizing drive is the most ambitious one ever undertaken in the high- technology sector, where the nation's labor movement has yet to establish a foothold.
>
> The Communications Workers of America has undertaken a campaign to unionize 400 customer-service representatives in Seattle, where Amazon is based. The United Food and Commercial Workers Union and the Prewitt Organizing Fund, an independent organizing group, are seeking

to unionize some 5,000 workers at Amazon's eight distribution centers across the country. The unionization drive has gained momentum because many workers are upset about layoffs at Amazon last January.

This evidence suggests that Amazon's bulletin on why 'a union is not desirable' can easily be compared to the problems of employee relations within the labour process reported by the abolition of the Dock Labour scheme (Turnbull and Weston 1993), or the dynamics of the insecure workforce (Blyton and Turnbull 1998; Turnbull and Wass 1997), as well as the use of marketing concepts and rhetoric to implement rationalization within the United Kingdom's National Health Service (Bailey et al. 2017). Greenhouse (2000) quotes an official Amazon spokesperson (Patty Smith) as saying that the material on the website was to assist supervisors on knowing what they can do to oppose a union and "what actions by managers violate laws barring retaliation against workers who support unionization". Indeed, it appears that the lived reality for many Amazon workers striving for productivity is, for example, not to take toilet breaks but rather relieve themselves into plastic bottles while working; such is their need to be seen to be productive which itself forms the focal point on Amazon within the pantheon of 'Bullshit Jobs' (Graeber 2018). Elsewhere, how best should we welcome the news that Yelles (2017) screams "Eco-Friendly Bombs: Insert Punchline here", which illustrates how progress is being made by scientists developing bombs that kill people but don't harm the environment.

Prefiguring critical marketing communications with the emergence of corporate sustainability

As Hackley 2019 has observed, regarding advertising, we also argue that care should be taken to reconsider what has been orchestrated in the production process for marketing communications (including CSR). With a rich resource base at their disposal, large multinational corporations are indeed *shaping* the very discourse around sustainability while academics still argue over the vagaries of definitions around sustainable consumption and production. Any prefiguration of corporate sustainability is restricted by the general publics' limited awareness that it is indeed at play. Early reviews suggest as much about managers' motivations for getting behind such change within organizations (Salzmann, Ionescu-somers, and Steger 2005). Many in society are happy to see organizations making truth claims about what they are doing in the name of the environment or how one organization claims how they are building sustainable brands. Within the management literature, there has been a suggestion that despite different past both CSR and corporate sustainability share a common future (Montiel 2008). Nonetheless, in the eyes of some critical macromarketers (Kilbourne McDonagh, and Prothero 2018, 597), these developments are best understood as the hegemonic process of capitalism reproducing itself; they suggest,

The fundamental problem in this hegemonic process (Gramsci, 1971) is that strong sustainability is incompatible with the prevailing meta-narrative that demands unlimited economic growth in a finite system. The end result of the hegemonic process is that a new myth about sustainability in the culture of consumption is created that factualises fictions (growth in consumption is the ultimate good) and fictionalises facts (current consumption practices are unsustainable). As both Marcuse (1963) and Gramsci (1971) argue, facts contrary to the major societal narrative are absorbed into the narrative rendering them impotent by transforming critique into naive acquiescence.

At a recent event in the British Academy (14 September 2018) received wisdom focussed on a difficult task of prefiguring activism (both academic and non-academic) during a time of increased awareness of the ecological crisis. Discussion ranged from the considered lived reality of the Occupy movement in London (Finsbury Park and St Pauls) to the interventions of what some are calling CEO or investor activism. At this arena, it was noted by Martin Parker that academics and individuals are constrained by the degree of activism in which they can engage, be it in their personal lives, in the workplace, or as citizens more generally. Taking a dictionary definition of the term, the ability to call to action is restricted by organizational norms and the requirements for academics to perform certain responsibilities within the institution settings in which they work. In this context, we need to be cautious when claims of activism and the CEO are being jointly discussed.

Ultimately, one can appreciate how strides to understand the organization have led to different perspectives on marketing communications, as noted in Figure 4.1 with moves from Point A to C, against various ongoing crises, but there seems to be little doubt that CSR and more lately corporate sustainability are attempts to depict a more caring and sharing organization when interacting with stakeholders. Their creations serve the organization as exercises in legitimation making. They appear to be very much 'extras', a case of marketing communications, the equivalent of the 'smiling salesperson' who is well briefed on the right things to say to the various publics to whom an organization sends messages. All of these developments ensure that organizations maintain their credibility and permission to continue doing business or 'Carry On' regardless. In this sense, corporate sustainability seems to be a perfect marriage of both the economic imperative and the ecological which we mentioned at the outset of this chapter in terms of sustainability. This happens at a time when corporations are positioning themselves are best placed to provide social and environmental solutions.

In this respect, the evolution of marketing communications has swiftly developed to include a number of communicative acts (including the pervasive use of social media), which underscore and uphold the market logic. Some writers such as Zwick and Dholokia (2008) and Arviddson (2008) have gone so far as to

───►

Communicative Acts:

    (A) Marketing Communications (MC)

    (including PR & Lobbying)

        (B) Integrated MC-> Corporate marketing

        CSR->

            (C) Corp sustainability->Murketing

On-going: Crises as triggers.

Outcomes: Organisational legitimacy – or permission to "Carry On' Regardless.

───►

FIGURE 4.1   Market logic supporting communicative acts across time.

argue that organizations using sophisticated information data capture and have turned people into 'co-producers' of value becoming more than just customers. In this sense, the organization has added new dimensions to the communicative act. Thus, to view marketing communications critically, one thus has to expand the original definitions to allow for the use of marketing to effect rationalization within the labour process (Delbridge 2006), the re-prioritization of enterprise values over those of trade unions (Lucio and West 1995), and the new sophistications of CSR (Crane and Glozer 2016), corporate sustainability, and sponsored social media as instrumental forms of messaging or communications which seek to maintain the legitimacy of the organization to continue operating or reclaim that space against a backdrop of litigation. This is worth ruminating over at length as to Marx (1848) one can truly say all that is solid melts into CSR or corporate sustainability. Given the rise of a digitalized network society whereby customers can use various social media tools to sing the praises of an organization in real time, via a twitter handle (Arvidsson and Caliandro 2016), it remains important for people to be able to read marketing communications that has corporate interests at their heart. Naturally, this ability to let people know how well or poorly an organization is performing requires swift communication by the organization to maintain its legitimacy and safeguard its reputation or to 'Carry On' regardless (Hatherley 2016). It is not uncommon for a marketing role to now include the management of social media and event management to guarantee return on investments. It would seem now more than ever we need to reconsider the need for sustainable communication to help people understand what organizations are communicating as part of the market logic. As Alder (1998) reflects on the need and acceptance of the polygraph in American society in helping discover those who lie, we submit that we need critical marketing communications to help unpack what Dunne (2018) calls 'Murketing' where in communicating there is open conceit and deceit deployed by organizations, often in a flirtatious manner, as a new form of organizational sincerity. We need this to discern the legitimate from the devious or misleading messaging that circulates in contemporary capitalism. Corporate power has long been challenged by social movements (Kozinets and Handelman 2004) and elements of society that require us to cross-check what has been communicated and why it has been communicated as a form of disingenuous persuasion.

Note

1 Dugan (2012, p1) outlines Baroness Orczy's hero thusly, "The global success of film and musical versions of The Scarlet Pimpernel have insured a place for this elusive hero in popular culture. His daring rescues are as much a part of the French Revolution as the howling mob and the toothless tricoteuses knitting at the foot of the guillotine. In many people's imaginations, he is Zorro crossed with Superman, with a dash of 18th-century elegance.

   As the mild-mannered man who shows one face to the world, but is secretly a man of action, the Scarlet Pimpernel has spawned a race of hidden heroes. Yet to his creator, Baroness Emmuska Orczy (1865–1947), he was something more: an English gentleman spreading English values among the benighted; an aristocrat rescuing aristocrats."

Bibliography

Adler, Ken (1998), "To Tell the Truth: The Polygraph Exam and the Marketing of American Expertise," *Historical Reflections*, 24(3), 487–525.

Arvidsson, Adam (2006), *Brands: Meaning and Value in Media Culture*, London: Routledge.

———— (2008), "The Ethical Economy of Customer Co-Production," *Journal of Macromarketing*, 28(4), 326–38.

Arvidsson, Adam and Alessandro Caliandro (2016), "Brand Public," *Journal of Consumer Research*, 42(5), 727–48.

Bailey, Simon, Kath Checkland, Damian Hodgson, Anne McBridge, Rebecca Elvey, Stephen Parkin, Katy Rothwell, and Dean Pierides (2017), "The Policy Work of Piloting: Mobilising and Managing Conflict and Ambiguity in the English NHS," *Social Science & Medicine*, 179, 210–17.

Balmer, John M. T. and Stephen A. Greyer (2006), "Corporate Marketing: Integrating Corporate Identity, Corporate Branding, Corporate Communications, Corporate Image and Corporate Reputation," *European Journal of Marketing*, 40(7/8), 730–41.

Blyton, Paul and Peter Turnbull (1998), *The Dynamics of Employee Relations*, 2nd edition, London: Macmillan Business.

Bradshaw, Alan, Pierre McDonagh, and David Marshall (2006), "No Space - New Blood and the Production of Brand Culture Colonies," *Journal of Marketing Management*, 22(5–6), 579–99.

Brammer, Stephen and Stephen Pavelin (2004), "Building a Good Reputation," *European Management Journal*, 22(6), 704–13.

Castells, Manuel (2009a), *Communication Power*, Oxford: Oxford University Press.

———— (2009b), *The Rise of the Network Society*, Vol. 1, Second Edition, Oxford: Blackwell.

Crane, Andrew and Sarah Glozer (2016), "Researching Corporate Social Responsibility Communication: Themes, Opportunities and Challenges: Researching CSR Communication," *Journal of Management Studies*, 53(7), 1223–52.

Crane, Andrew, Dirk Matten, and Laura Spence (2008), *Corporate Social Responsibility: Readings and Cases in a Global Context*, Abingdon, Oxon: Routledge.

Delbridge, Rick (2006), "Exetended Review: The Vitality of Labour Process Analysis," *Organization Studies*, 27(8), 1209–19.

Devereaux, J. (2012), "A Sustainability Academic Externship Pilot: A Unique Collaborative Project," *Sustainability: The Journal of Record*, 5(5), 305–10.

Dunne, Stephen (2008), "Corporate Social Responsibility and the Value of Corporate Moral Pragmatism," *Culture and Organization*, 14(2), 135–49.

Firat, A. Fuat, Lisa Peñaloza, and Alladi Venkatesh (2014), "The Market as a Sign System and the Logic of the Market," in *The Service Dominant Logic of Marketing*, London: Routledge, 269–83.

Fortson, Danny (2019), "Jeff Bezos Has Got a Problem with Unions at Amazon," *The Sunday Times*. Retrieved January 7, 2020 (https://www.thetimes.co.uk/article/jeff-bezos-has-got-a-problem-with-unions-at-amazon-wl8zhgscn).

Gabriel, Y. (2000), *Storytelling in Organizations: Facts, Fictions, and Fantasies: Facts, Fictions, and Fantasies*, Oxford: OUP.

Galvin, Ray. (2020), "Power, Evil and Resistance in Social Structure: A Sociology for Energy Research in a Climate Emergency," *Energy Research & Social Science*, 61, 101361

Goldman, Robert and Stephen Papson (1994), "Advertising in the Age of Hypersignification," *Theory, Culture & Society*, 11(3), 23–53.

———— (1996), *Sign Wars*, New York: Guilford.

Graeber, David (2018), *Bullshit Jobs: A Theory*, London: Allen Lane.

Greenhouse, Steven (2000), "US: Amazon.Com Fights Union Activity | Corpwatch," *CorpWatch*. Retrieved January 7, 2020 (https://corpwatch.org/article/us-amazoncom-fights-union-activity).

Hackley, Chris (2019), "Advertising Practice and Critical Marketing," in *The Routledge Companion to Critical Marketing*, eds. M. Tadajewski, M. Higgins, J. Denigri-Knott, and R. Varman, London: Routledge, 185–95.

Hatherley, Owen (2016), *The Ministry of Nostalgia*. London: Verso.

Hietanen, Joel, Mikael Andéhn, and Alan Bradshaw (2018), "Against the Implicit Politics of Service-Dominant Logic," *Marketing Theory*, 18(1), 101–19.

iSpot.TV. (2019), "Amazon TV Commercial, 'Work Hard,'" *ISpot.Tv*. Retrieved January 7, 2020 (http://www.ispot.tv/ad/ovXp/amazon-work-hard).

Karp, P. (2019), "Scott Morrison Returns from Holiday and Signals No Change to Climate Policy despite Bushfires Crisis." *The Guardian*, December 22.

Keller, Kevin Lane (2009), "Building Strong Brands in a Modern Marketing Communications Environment," *Journal of Marketing Communications*, 15(2–3), 139–55.

Kilbourne, William E. (2004), "Sustainable Communication and the Dominant Social Paradigm: Can They Be Integrated?" *Marketing Theory*, 4(3), 187–208.

Kilbourne, William E. et al. (2009), "The Institutional Foundations of Material in Western Societies," *Journal of Macromarketing*, 29(3), 259–78.

Kilbourne, William E., Pierre McDonagh, and Andrea Prothero (2018), "Sustainable Consumption, Consumer Culture and the Politics of a Megatrend," in *The SAGE Handbook of Consumer Culture*, eds. O. Kravets, P. Maclaran, S. Miles, and A. Venkatesh, London: SAGE.

Kozinets, Robert V. and Jay M. Handelman (2004), "Adversaries of Consumption: Consumer Movements, Activism, and Ideology," *The Journal of Consumer Research*, 31(3), 691–704.

L'Etang, Jacquie (1994), "Public Relations and Corporate Social Responsibility: Some Issues Arising," *Journal of Business Ethics*, 13(1), 111–23.

———— (2005), "Critical Public Relations: Some Reflections," *Public Relations Review*, 31(4), 521–26.

L'Etang, Jacquie, David McKie, Nancy Snow, and Jordi Xifra, eds. (2015),. *The Routledge Handbook of Critical Public Relations*. London: Routledge.

Loftus, Peter (2020), "For First Time, CEO Testifies in a Talcum-Powder Court Case," https://www.wsj.com/articles/for-first-time-j-j-ceo-testifies-in-a-talcum-powder-court-case-11580161175, accessed 2 Feb 2020.

Lucio, Miguel M. and Weston, Syd. (1995), "Trade Unions and Networking in the Context of Change: Evaluating the Outcomes of Decentralization in Industrial Relations," *Economic and Industrial Democracy*, 16(2), 233–51.

Marx, Karl and Friedrich Engels (1848), *The Communist Manifesto*, London: Penguin.

McDonagh, Pierre (1995), "Sustainable Communication: Pipe Dream for Green Advertisers or the New Way for Business to Communicate," in *Marketing Today and for the 21st Century: Proceedings of the 24th European Marketing Academy Conference*, 731–51.

———— (1998), "Towards a Theory of Sustainable Communication in Risk Society: Relating Issues of Sustainability to Marketing Communication," *Journal of Marketing Management*, 14(6), 591–622.

———— (2002), "Communicative Campaigns to Effect Anti-Slavery and Fair Trade: The Cases of Rugmark and Cafedirect." *European Journal of Marketing*, 36(5/6), 642–66.

McDonagh, Pierre, William E. Kilbourne, and Andrea Prothero (2014), "Re-Affirming the Prevailing Order?" in *Humanistic Marketing*, eds. R. E. Varey. London: Palgrave Macmillan, 29–38.

McDonagh, Pierre and Andrea Prothero (2015), "Unpacking Corporate Sustainability," in *Waste Management and Sustainable Consumption*, London: Routledge, 166–83.

McGranahan, Carole (2016), "Theorizing Refusal: An Introduction," *Cultural Anthropology*, 31(3), 319–325.

Meneo, Ron (2020), "Talcum Powder Lawsuits," *Consumer Safety*, The Meneo Law Group, https://www.consumersafety.org/product-lawsuits/talcum-powder/, accessed 2 Feb 2020.

Montiel, Ivan (2008), "Corporate Social Responsibility and Corporate Sustainability: Separate Pasts, Common Futures," *Organization & Environment*, 21(3), 245–69.

Mullen, Andrew (2010), "Twenty Years on: The Second-Order Predictons of the Herman-Chomsky Propaganda Model," *Media, Culture & Society*, 32(4), 673–90.

Nair, Arathy S. (2017), "DuPont Settles Lawsuits over Leak of Chemical used to Make Teflon," Reuters, https://www.reuters.com/article/us-du-pont-lawsuit-west-virginia-idUSKBN15S18U, accessed 2 Feb 2020.

O'Kelly, Emma (2019), "Higgins Critical of Universities focus on Markets," *Radio TelifIs Eireann RTE*, 30th Sept. https://www.rte.ie/news/education/2019/0930/1079255-michael-d-higgins/, accessed 2 Feb 2020.

Olah, Nathalie (2019), "Of Course Facebook and Google Want to 'Solve' Social Problems. They're Hungry for Our Data | Nathalie Olah." *The Guardian*, December 2.

Salzmann, Oliver, Aileen Ionescu-somers, and Ulrich Steger (2005), "The Business Case for Corporate Sustainability: Literature Review and Research Options," *European Management Journal*, 23(1), 27–36.

Schroeder, Jonathan (2002), *Visual Consumption*, London: Routledge.

Sustainable Brands (2019), "Sustainable Brands," https://sustainablebrands.com/, accessed 5 May 2019.

Tadajewski, Mark and Douglas Brownlie (2009), "Critical Marketing: A Limit Attitude," in *Critical Marketing: Issues in Contemporary Marketing*, eds. M. Tadajewski and D. Brownlie. London: Wiley.

The Sustainable SME (2012), Dec 7th https://thesustainablesme.com/2012/12/07/sustainnext-we-need-to-act-now-on-sustainability/, accessed 2 Feb 2020.

Turnbull, Peter and Victoria Wass (1997), "Job Insecurity and Labour Market Lemons: The (Mis)Management of Redundancy in Stell Making, Coal Mining and Port Transport," *Journal of Managment Studies*, 34(1), 27–51.

Turnbull, Peter and Syd Weston (1993), "The British Port Transport Industry Part 2. Employment, Working Practices and Productivity," *Maritime Policy & Management*, 20(3), 181–95.

Williamson, J. (1978), *Decoding Advertisements: Ideology and Meaning in Advertising*, London: Marion Boyers.

Woodside, A.G., Sood, S. and Miller, K.E. (2008), "When Consumers and Brands Talk: Storytelling theory and research in psychology and marketing," *Psychology & Marketing*, 25(2), 97–145.

Wolfe-Robinson, Maya (2019), "Union Stages Final Protest over 'horrific' Amazon Work Practices," *The Guardian*, July 22.

Yelles, William (2017), "Eco-Friendly Bombs: Insert Punchline here," *Pacific Standard*, https://psmag.com/economics/eco-friendly-bombs-insert-punchline-here-4511, accessed 2 Feb 2020.

Zwick, Detlev and Julien Cayla, eds. (2011), *Inside Marketing: Practices, Ideologies, Devices*, Oxford: Oxford University Press.

Zwick, Detlev and Nikhilesh Dholakia (2008), "Infotransformation of Markets: Introduction to the Special Issue on Marketing and Information Technology," *Journal of Macromarketing*, 28(4), 318–25.

5

SUCCESS, STATUS, AND THE LOGIC OF INDIVIDUALISM

Introduction

Despite predictions that the Global Financial Crisis would bring about a new era of income equality and more socially-minded measures of status and what it is to live a meaningful life (Birdsall and Fukuyama 2011), success within globalized capitalism is still encapsulated by an individual's rise to dizzy heights of wealth accumulation. Freed from obligations to others, disembedded from civic society, and drunk on mythologies of self-reliance and self-willed wealth, entrepreneurs' status in society remains unquestioned. When criticism is levelled at Elon Musk and Jeff Bezos, appealing to sacrosanct values of individual wealth and individual achievement allows them to proceed with their questionable business practices relatively unimpeded. And as Amazon's recently filed patents that show the company's plan to colonize unused reservoirs and the skies with autonomous delivery vehicles (Walter 2017), the individual entrepreneur is someone who believes the world should be shaped in their image, as if the natural world is something that can be controlled and coerced in the pursuit of individual wealth accomulation.

The super-rich have houses in cities such as London, New York, Hong Kong, and San Francisco, and have boltholes on islands or in secluded rural estates. These people are not connected to the nations that granted them their opportunities; they are 'global nomads' (Bardhi, Eckhardt, and Arnould 2012) whose global wealth allows them to take private flights, avoid tax, and exist outside normal constraints set by society. This is to say that the decline in inquality that some predicted in the aftermatch of the GFC did not happen. In 2017, an Oxfam report claimed that the eight billionaires own as much combined wealth as the poorest half of the human race. Not that the super-rich are sympathetic to those who are struggling. As Mihail Kkodorovsky, once Russian's richest man, once said to journalist Chrystia Freeland (2011), "If a man is not an oligarch, something is not right with him … Everyone had the same starting conditions, everyone could have done it".

In this chapter, we mine the logic of individualism further. In doing so, we return to work from the 1960s to expose how 'possessive individualism' (Macpherson 1962) is entrenched in contemporary consumer culture and call into question dominant representations of success, hedonism, and the myth of the 'entrepreneurial ubermensch'. We then explore recent attempts to reclaim the individual subject as an agent of emancipatory social change. We finally note the challenge for critical marketing communications if we are to build social alternatives not rooted in individual material abundance and wealth accumulation.

Individualism and capitalism

Individualism lies at the heart of American and European cultures (Lukes 1971). Despite having distinct histories and meanings across these regions and countries, individualism emphasizes the "right to selfhood, the right to privacy, and the freedom to fully develop potential, unimpeded by societal barrers" (Hirschman 2003, 10). But the form of individualism indissolubly tied to liberal democracy and globalized capitalism valorizes an entrepreneurial-self that sees no ties or obligations to others and an individual consumer who is free to find pleasure and identity in any form of consumption experience (Firat and Venkatesh 1995). Central institutions and rights associated with advanced capitalist societies exist to service autonomous property-owning individuals and risk-taking entrepreneurs (Beck and Beck-Gernsheim 2002), and the diversification of markets, coupled with businesses' capacity to customize and individualize commodities at little cost, means that businesses nowadays offer something for everybody.

A capitalism where everyone has a part to play. In contrast to received wisdom, marketing does not just simply discover wants, desires, and needs but works to actively develop them. Consumer culture's focus on sweetening the wants of an individual is a recurring trope. The Fordist factory of mass production no longer exists, and the leading edge of marketing and product development are methods and practices through which firms co-opt consumers as co-designers (Cova and Dalli 2009; Streeck 2017; Zwick, Bonsu, and Darmody 2008). Consumers are 'empowered' (Shankar, Cherrier, and Canniford 2006) to contribute with enthusiasm to test new products and develop new ideas, and are encouraged to play on firm-owned platforms, where the material and immaterial fruits of their labour can be transformed into viable products and services (Cova and Dalli 2009; Thrift 2008). But technological advances cannot be overlooked, particularly the advent proflieration and monetization of social media (Andzulis, Panagopoulos and Rapp, 2012), since they are key to forms of biopolitical marketing, which, as Zwick and Bradshaw (2016, 94) explain,

> aims to mobilize and extract value from the production of consumer communication, lifestyles and subjectivities. It is a vision of marketing that

wants to replace the conventional ethos of consumer discipline and control with an ethos of the network; emphasizing openness and non-hierarchical collaboration, autonomy, and harmonious social production. Biopolitical marketing rejects any clear distinction between marketer and consumer and sees marketing as deeply inserted into, and increasingly indistinguishable from, the fabric of everyday life.

Here, it is not simply that marketers look to place consumers somewhere in the chain of new product development. Instead, the virtual communities that develop in social media spaces are inseparable from commercial interests and value production activities. Consumers are therefore encouraged to express themselves, and their creative capacities are then channelled into the production of new products, lifestyles, and aesthetics (Zwick and Bradshaw 2016). Within 'the fabric of everyday life', the immediate extraction of value from social networks perpetuates this logic of individualism, convincing atomized individuals that they have 'value' and can create value in contemporary society.

Following Paul Virilio's work Open Sky, which considers the social destruction wrought by information technology and the global media, it is possible to reflect on the world of marketing dominated by social networks. In Virilio's view, hyper-information existence facilitated by technologies of ubiquity, virtuality, and instantaneity is not a liberating state of affairs. Instead, such existence entraps people in a 'gray ecology', robbing them of colour, of the possibility of spatial distancing, and of rooted sensory perception. This occurs 24/7 with the need to be 'always connected to the internet' that mobile technology ensures (Crary 2013). Our preoccupation with the need to find Wi-Fi wherever we are is just one indication of this, as is the roll-out of 5G networking, which promises unprecedented speed for users. But beyond the development of a form of capitalism that blurs the boundaries between producer and consumer, and can extract value from us whether we like it or not, the logic of individualism is also crucial in obscuring the harmful effects of globalized capitalism.

Possessive individualism. The championing of individualism is part and parcel of how advanced capitalist societies have helped obscure the impact of global production chains and the consequence of acts of individual consumption on others. As we discussed in Chapter 2, globalized capitalism has seen ecology be eclipsed by hyper-consumption (Kilbourne et al. 1997). The logic of 'possessive individualism' (Macpherson 1962) is the key that pervades this process of being free from obligations to others. For this reason, Little (2018) asks us to remember that possessive individualism and conservative liberation groups are close bedfellows, where

> The Tea Party seems to be a contemporary descendant of this ideology. Taxation is theft; the state has no legitimate role beyond protecting individual security and property; government regulation of private business activity is an immoral intrusion on liberty and property; individuals possess

liberties and property that the state cannot limit; individuals deserve what they own and owe nothing to society or other citizens. Justice is served by simply protecting the possessions of individual citizens.

By extension, the market offers individuals blind to the harms associated with one's consumption habits as the ultimate in self-centred consumption and self-expression. Narcissists it seems prefer online communities based on shallow relationships where they can exercise control (Sheldon and Bryant 2016), and males and females can shop for 'people' with whom they can share their most intimate experiences. For example, a person travelling in the United States, Europe, or Australia can check out 'paid-for companionship' ranging from cheap massages with 'happy endings' to more risky sexual encounters almost anywhere. People advertise their personal services online (see Castle and Lee, 2008) and on mainstream classified advertisement sites such as Craigslist, Vivastreet, or Gumtree, and on specific escort sites that personalize offers based on the location of the individual. People, some of whom are enslaved, are offered to the individual with an exoticized menu of nationalities, sexual preferences, price rates, and special offers. The market encourages the individual not to self-gratify but to have an affair instead despite the concern over data leaks of its users (see Lobera et al. 2020). This darker effect of the mass personalization of service is a phenomenon witnessed across the globe as the industrialization of prostitution has created a multibillion market sector (Jeffreys 2009), the result of the merging of sexual freedom and consecration of possessive individualism, combined with the legalization of prostitution in many countries around the world.

'Possessive individualism' also refers to the idea that the individual as "solely an owner of himself … for which he owes nothing to society" (Macpherson 1962, 264) means that the breaking of social ties and moral obligations to others. This also means buying into the ideology of full-self reliance and self-esteem, in which strength and resolve can see you overcome any obstacle (Greene 2008). This 'possessive individualism' is at the centre of Tocqueville's (1835, 104–105) description of America's strand of individualism when he observed that Americans "owe nothing to any man; they expect nothing from any man; they acquire the habit of always considering themselves as standing alone, and are apt to imagine that their whole destiny is in their own hands".

The self-serving logic of possessive individualism has become so taken for granted that the phrase 'survival of the fittest' pervades our understanding of social life (Gimeno et al. 1997; Zingales 1998; Solomon et al. 2013). Those who thrive under pressure, or excel in competition, are held in high regard by their equally high-achieving peers and are seen by those who are less well off, or perceived as being less worthy, as 'having it all'. These characters are often depicted on the big-screen successful characters like Gordon Gecko in *Wall Street* or more recently by Di Caprio's Jordan Belfort in *Wolf of Wall Street* whose efforts to show others how to amass personal fortunes encapsulate the essence of contemporary possessive individualism. Indeed, even today Jordan Belfort's character still attracts the adulation of many writers such as Dineen (2019) for his staying power and ability to continue to amass wealth. This is a remarkable achievement given that as a 56-year bankrupt who has survived drug addiction, gaol, he is depicted as someone in good health who can pass on wisdom, helping you close that sale, as long as you are willing to pay a monthly subscription. This is not, however, simply embelamtic of the worst traits of American culture.

To say such possessive individualism remains the pursuit of a few elitists in society is a gross oversimplification of how much the desire for material wealth presently also pervades European societies. The reader should consider how widespread use of marketing communications encourages gambling, for example, on the 'EuroMillions' lottery, where the advertising hails people with the prospect of having millions to spend 'as a nicer problem to have'. The focus in these advertisements is on choosing which tropical island to own, blind to ecological harm, ignorant of waste. Although lottery organizers do support charitable causes, lottery winnings are nevertheless framed in terms of the prospect of individual wealth and the potential for material abundance (Moore 1997).

Lauding the entrepreneurial ubermensch

But not everyone has to turn to EuroMillions to strike it rich, and of course not every Jordan Belfort is brought down to earth. In the light of criticism of globalized capitalism's capacity to provide adequate standing of living for everyone, marketing communications has found value in lauding what we conceptualize as the 'entrepreneurial ubermensch' figure. The entrepreneurial ubermensch is not someone who is born to wealth and priviledge, but is self-made. The entrepreneurial ubermensch is the embodiment of the 'American Dream' (Hochschild 1996) which sees individuals rise from humble beginnings to amass monetary wealth. And like Nietzsche's (2006) concept of the ubermensch, the entrepreneurial ubermensch stands above the business world and others in it, willfully ignorant of morality and compassion, and derives pleasure in violating norms and social mores in the pursuit of capital accumulation. While the majority may see crises and emergenices, they see market opportunities instead (Calthorpe 1993). The entrepreneurial ubermensch does not seek public acceptance but takes pleasure in moving the world in a direction of their choosing.

At the height of summer 2019, as this book is being written, one contemporary example encapsulates the naked ambition of the entrepreneurial ubermensch. Situated high above the ground a giant 100-meter-tall advert hangs in Ireland's Terminal 2 of Dublin Airport epitomizing *success*, this in a country still scarred by 11 years of austerity following the banking crisis of 2008. It depicts a 'gifted' young male business person, suit and tie, gazing sideways against the backdrop of a dawning modern metropolis, a person who works for or is assisted by Bank of America Merrill Lynch, being appellated with the tagline of 'The Power to take on tomorrow, what would you like the power to do?' Here, a man stands above us, in the clouds, where the metropolis built to service capital is his dominion. This business person takes delight in their superiority over others and takes pity on the weak.

The mythic quality of the entrepreneurial ubermensch has developed through the popularity of the reality television show *The Apprentice*. Licensed across 17 different countries and now in its fifteenth series in the United Kingdom, the program offers people the chance of an investment of £250,000 and 50:50 partnership with the businessman Lord Sugar. Sugar is your archetypal 'East-End barrow boy made good' (McGuigan 2008, 315) who uses his just-as-repellent advisors to bark orders and humiliate contestants who you should be sympathetic towards if they weren't as obnoxious. Regardless, individuals are challenged by the program's advertising with the tagline 'Could you be the next big thing?' and encouraged to "show us what you've got" with the besuited Lord Sugar standing in front of the City of London, arms folded, waiting to be convinced of your business case. Couldry and Littler (2011, 267) argue that the show itself is an exemplar of 'neoliberal governmentality' as it naturalizes a particular view of individual power, will, and lack of responsibility for others. They observe that

> the UK version of *The Apprentice* shows more obviously the *tensions behind* neoliberalism's impoverishment of the social, tensions also reflected in New Labour's particular political translation of international neoliberal doctrine (Hall, 2003): this is the Britain where more than half of managers were shown in a recent survey to suffer ill-health through overwork (Chartered Management Institute, 2006), and a majority of managers saw their belief in the importance of enjoying their work to be at odds with their employers' view (Chartered Management Institute, 2007), while at the very top, the average UK chief executive is paid 100 times more than the average worker in their organization (*Guardian*, 2 October 2006). The UK programme's myth of 'hard-won' celebrity surely has a role in negotiating those tensions.

Of note also here is that the individual is praised for being able to withstand aggressiveness by Sir Alan in any cross-examination, whereas being able to work in a group carries less attraction. As Couldry and Littler (2011, 273) write, "Good work within a group, it is implied, counts for *nothing at all* beside the ability to satisfy Sir Alan in direct confrontation". This confrontation takes place in a boardroom that could be in any financial centre in the world. Little sense is spoken in these confrontations, where what is being tested is one's capacity to take a verbal beating and schmooze their way out of the boardroom without being told that they are 'fired'.

For much political theory, individuals appear as a particular type of personhood that stands in the way of emancipatory social and economic change. For radical change to come about, other kinds of personhood rooted in non-individualist modes of thought that uphold values of solidarity and appreciate the interdependency of human life upon others and the natural world (Gilbert 2014). However, in the next section, we explore recent ideas concerning how individuals can pursue emancipatory social and economic change.

Reclaiming the individual subject as a source of emancipation

Of late, market theorists Fuat Firat and Niklesh Dholakia (2017) have begun to prefigure an individual political subjectivity rooted in technological and cultural changes. For them it is vital that any radically different future rests on the development of a subjectivity that is geared towards providing blueprints for alternative ways of living:

> We would suggest that this human subject might be that of the construer, the being that transcends the entrenched consumer, is able and willing to participate in mythologies and, based on these myths, to construe organizations of life without much regard for representation or reflection of "what is,' especially 'what is (commercially) branded' into our consciousness. Transcending the self-referential, self-reproducing character of the iconographic culture, the construer subject may be expected to focus on contributing to a culture of presenting the possible and the potential. A wider recognition of the fact that humanity constructs its environment more so than takes it as a given will license the construer to focus on 'what is possible' rather than 'what is.' When what is already experienced is not taken as a given, not accepted as an inviolate material condition, but is understood to be the construction of a symbolic culture, there is a chance to imagine what can be and to transform the world.
>
> *(Firat and Dholakia 2017, 515)*

Firat and Dholakia argue that human subjectivity has varied over time, with the dominant current form being the *consumer* which supplanted the original concept of the *citizen*. They claim that for meaningful tangible and material change to occur in the future, we need to encourage forms of education and socialization that enables the development of a *construer* subjectivity which at least allows for the conditions to be in place to transform our world away from possessive individualism and towards the common good (see Table 5.1).

Democratizing technological means of production. Central to their argument is that the technological tools capable of producing emancipatory change are now under greater democratic control. They argue that technological developments – three-dimensional printing, open-source design, and the machines that continue to improve in their capabilities annual – have helped to bring the conditions through which the constuer is formed, explaining that

> Several emergent new concepts – indeed, more than just concepts, actual processes and methods such as produsage, participatory design, digital prosumption democratic innovation, the 'maker movement', and user-generated manufacturing are paving the way for the new construer subjectivity to take hold. The maker movement, for example, traces its history to hobbyists and tinkerers but has embraced advanced aspects of digital technology and a social ethic of sharing and helping.
>
> *(Firat and Dholakia 2017, 515–16)*

TABLE 5.1 Changing concepts of human subjectivity – Citizen, Consumer, Construer

Subjectivity	Traditional to modern society	Modern to Late Modern	Late Modern to present	Characteristics
Citizen	Citizen – civil rights, liberties, and equalities for communities			Culture anchored to faith
Consumer		Consumer – marketized individualism and brand empires		Culture based on materialism and marketization
Construer			Construer – collaborative knowledge management and artistic creation Learner-led education and citizen engaged in politics	Iconographic culture

Firat and Dholakia's argument is novel, since they treat technological change as harbouring radical potential. They suggest that underlying these technological changes that place the means of production in the hands of ordinary consumers is also the revival of a more socially minded and non-individualist ethos (see also Srnicek and Williams 2016). For these are indeed communities informed by open participation, common property rights, and collaborative creation, and so on. This is in contrast with other theorizations that see similar technological changes as exacerbating some of the most harmful tendencies of globalized capitalism. With the rise of the Internet and a network society (Castells 2000, 2007, 2011), there is greater potential for much more connectivity than before. As Castells (2007, 246) explains,

> The communication foundation of the network society is the global web of horizontal communication networks that include the multimodal exchange of interactive messages from many to many both synchronous and asynchronous. Of course, the Internet is an old technology, first deployed in 1969. But it is only in the last decade that reached out throughout the world to exceed now 1 billion users. Mobile communication has exploded

reaching over 2 billion mobile phone subscribers in 2006 in contrast to 16 million in 1991. So, even accounting for the differential diffusion in developing countries and poor regions, a very high proportion of the population of the planet has access to mobile communication, sometimes in areas where there is no electricity but there is some form of coverage and mobile chargers of mobile batteries in the form of merchant bicycles. Wifi and wimax networks are helping to set up networked communities. With the convergence between Internet and mobile communication and the gradual diffusion of broadband capacity, the communicating power of the Internet is being distributed in all realms of social life, as the electrical grid and the electrical engine distributed energy in the industrial society.

One impact of the 'Internet being distributed in all realms of social life' is that our connection with others and the way in which they converse has dramatically changed, and there is a case to make it is not for the better. While social networking sites promise new forms of communication and community – Facebook's mission statement used to be "making the world more open and connected" (Lanchester 2017) – their use makes people feel lonier and more isolated (Turkle 2011). For a generation of young people, though social media tends to be the place, they go to bear their soul to the world. The notion of the construer stands against this technological pessimism, and instead treats technological change as providing the tools for radical change, but also reigniting a utopian imagination.

Building new symbolic cultures. Firat and Dholakia also attribute the construer's radical potential to cultural changes. Consumers' creative potential means that they can form radical 'symbolic cultures' (Firat and Dholakia 2017, 516). Marketing and consumer research highlights how symbolic cultures transform everyday practices into magical experiences, reenchanting ordinary activities such as drinking beer, baking, or driving (Belk and Costa 1998; Godelier 2020; Holt 2004; Holt and Thompson 2004). However, these are all symbolic cultures predominantly created by marketers for consumers to live through. However, Firat and Dholakia stress that creative consumers have the capacity to produce new signs, creating new 'symbolic cultures' through the constellation of new signs, not relying on the codes and mythic stories provided by marketers. The future, they predict, will involve the constuer being a

> conflicted and stressed figure – attempting to write the script of participatory innovation, collaorative design, and democratic production and distribution on the (hopefully fading) palimpsest of powerful financescapes and brandscapes. ... The construer will have to be continually alert and innovative to overcome the paradox of striving to be an autonomous symbol-producer-and-sharer in an ultra-potent, capitalist, iconographic brandscape.
>
> *(Firat and Dholakia 2017, 518)*

Art, symbolic culture, and critique

In this way, Firat and Dholakia are following in the tradition that sees one source of emancipatory change lying in the development of art and symbolism. Across all epochs – pre-modern, modern, and late modern – artists help us better understand changes in human subjectivity or construe, expose, or start to question the prevailing order and reflect on what humanity has become and raise consciousness of marketing as ideology (Eckhardt, Varman, and Dholakia 2019). If we consider and then extrapolate what Iain Biggs (2019) suggests about the critical nature of art and the work of artists,

> What is the nature of the work such artists produce if not an expression of the culture of possessive individualism, the global economics the culture feeds and is fed by, and the deepening epistemological crisis in which current presuppositions about creativity are embedded? And that's clear even before we link these things to an environmental situation that, in all probability, is now nearing its terrible endgame.

Of course, art isn't always critical, and the artists can find themselves co-opted by marketers and ambitious brands (Delphine and Arnould 2011; Joy et al. 2014). Art, for instance, can perpetuate the culture of possessive individualism. Keith Alexander's BBC's *Outing Art* documentary of 1992 outlined the uncomfortable close and troubled relationship between the world of art and the world of advertising with pop artist Richard Hamilton, arguing that it will be art that people use to historically decipher what is occurring in society not advertising. Advertisers continually raid the referent system of artists to sell us more stuff, but many contemporary artists resist the commercial appropriation of their work. Consider the response of contemporary Chinese artist and activist Ai Weiwei (2019) whose work was used by the German car manufacturer Volkswagen. He asserts,

> I created Soleil Levant especially for World Refugee Day in 2017. It was exhibited on Kunsthal Charlottenborg's external facade from 20 June to 1 October 2017. The installation was used as the backdrop for an orange VW Polo without my knowledge or permission by a company that imports Volkswagens into Denmark. These actions are clear violations of my intellectual property and moral rights, but more importantly they raise larger questions of corporate power and responsibility in our era of global capitalism…This is not simply a case about copyright infringement. It is an opportunity to re-examine our understanding of justice and the responsibilities of individuals and corporations…My experience with Volkswagen is one small reflection of this broader lack of concern for the rights of individuals. The fact the company sees its future as one of partnership with an authoritarian regime speaks volumes. For my part, I will do what I can to ensure

that its commercial partners understand that no matter how powerful it becomes, there will always be those who insist on holding it to account.

It is here in both these artist interventions that we see the realization of Richard Hamilton's claim that artists are at the forefront of alerting and informing people about what is happening in society and his assertion that historians will turn to art for reading society, rather than reading adverts of any epoch to truly assess what was occurring in society.

Such work lays the foundations for what we submit is required to read marketing communications critically. In this regard, the techniques of art criticism need to be re-applied to current modes of marketing communications to enable construal by the subject. Consider how Elena Martinique explains how art criticism itself came into being:

> Art criticism likely originated with the origins of art itself, as evidenced by texts found in the works of Plato, Vitruvius or St. Augustine among others. It can be broadly defined as a discussion and interpretation of art and its value, in the pursuit of a rational basis for art appreciation. In 1932, the French poet and philosopher Paul Valéry defined art criticism as *"a form of literature which condenses or amplified, emphasizes or arranges or attempts to bring into harmony all the ideas that come to the mind when it is confronted by artistic phenomena"*, with a domain extending *"from metaphysics to invective"*. Interpretative analysis and aesthetical judgments dominated the discourse of art criticism for a long period of time, and art criticism has been an inevitable part of contemporary art dynamics. The criticism has an important role in developing and deepening the work of artists, but also in helping viewers perceive, and interpret works of art.

In this spirit, critical marketing communications needs to engage and draw together the tools of political, feminist, and social analysis, history, theory, and storytelling to expose the tropes within contemporary communicative acts on behalf of marketing. Additionally, we suggest that any radical alternative to globalized capitalism needs to consider ways of rethinking our relationship to material possessions.

Materialism in the dominant social paradigm

The logic of individualism plays a pivotal role in the values orientation of materialism (Kilbourne et al. 2009). Materialism occurs within and as a result of the institutions that prop up and maintain competitive markets. Four aspects of a competitive market of particular importance are private property, atomized buyers and sellers, a medium of exchange, and information. Materialism within the dominant social paradigm as a system has been shown to be structured (Kilbourne et al. 2009) following five dimensions: economic, technological, political, organizational (ecocentric vs. anthropocentric), and functional (cooperative vs. competitive) and their collective influence on materialism.

By way of a quick summary here of this work let us consider the main arguments within the *political dimension*. Locke (1963) proposes the main principles that characterize the political institutions of contemporary Western societies to be possessive individualism, private property, and limited government. As Kilbourne et al. (2009) note, possessive individuals are free from the will of others, enter into social relations voluntarily, and are the sole proprietors of their capacities and the product of their labour, which in turns leads to the legitimation of private property.

Within the *economic dimension*, there is a mutual reinforcing logic of the need for buyers and sellers. Growth within markets is based on an impersonal ideal of resource allocation. There are key important issues at play within the economic dimension, which has dominated much management scholarship and left a dull impression on neo-classical marketing. There individuals are free to pursue their interest as they see it, the definition of progress is coterminous with increased consumption, and finally, the maldistribution of wealth is justified by the efficiency criterion referred to as Pareto optimality. This once more requires increased consumption and growth so one human's gain is not at the expense of others.

Within the *technological dimension*, the prevailing attitude towards technology is one of unrestrained optimism towards further development (Ehrenfeld 1978). This attitude is completely justified so long as the criterion for social success is defined as material progress. Indeed, technological optimism is now fairly widespread so much so that the political, economic, and technological dimensions are mutually reinforcing. Programmes such as the BBC's Tomorrows World are worth reconsidering to understand the techno-optimist, as is the four-part documentary *Virtual Revolution* presented by the Guardian's Technology writer Aleks Krotoski broadcast on BBC Two on 30 January 2010. This co-production between the BBC and the Open University predominantly looks at the impact the World Wide Web has had since its inception 20 years ago; its access to the main protagonists on the tech revolution unmasks the hidden hands of the free market and the subsequent militaristic appropriation of what was initially a more liberal ethos behind the manifesto for cyberspace.

Within the *organizational (anthropocentric) dimension*, there is a dominant view that nature is a resource for humankind, and, along with a mechanical worldview, such 'humancentredness' is founded upon the idea that human survival requires mastery over nature (Merchant 1980), thus creating an anthropocentric society that overrides past, more respectful, views of nature.

Within the *functional (competitive) dimension*, a market-based society requires continuous competition among members for interminably scarce resources (Hobbes 1950). As a consequence, individual well-being turns from interest in social relations to interest in material possessions (Donaldson and Werhane 1993). This interpersonal competition is only limited by natural resources available and produces unequal wealth but again is reinforced by the other dimensions of the dominant social paradigm. Once again this underscores the widespread 'taken-for-granted' understanding of market society as some type of dog-eat-dog world. We note this manifests in marketing communications that naturalizes private health insurance, in a society hard pressed for public healthcare, such as for the company BUPA, one of the company's adverts for private healthcare insurance tells the person concerned with mental health well-being "So whatever's on your mind, it's normal to us". As such the concerned individual or their family knows that for satisfactory healthcare, the private route is more competitive and reassuring and relying on the public healthcare system.

As Kilbourne et al. (2009, 265) argue, "Within this type of society, materialism appears natural as the rewards to be achieved in the competition are material rewards, and attaining them legitimizes both the competitive individual pursuit and the system that produces them". In the light of this work, one should not underestimate any return to the human subjectivity and the challenges facing the construer in the dominant social paradigm. Efforts must begin to enable several things:

1 A concerted effort by the society's leaders to effectively characterize zero economic growth as a positive outcome.
2 Modifying cultural values that endorse self-enhancement to ones that accept the notion of sacrificing one's individual freedom for societal well-being.
3 Privileging ecosystem integrity over business decisions, which in turn means recognizing that competition, while increasing societal well-being at some levels of development, can become destructive of both resources and societal well-being if allowed to flourish in other historical contexts.

Given the timescale over which the dominant social paradigm has consolidated the logic of individualism and the ensuing desire for material possessions, Firat and Dholakia's (2017) *construer* subject's first step is to make consumers 'code conscious' (Holt 2002; Murray and Ozanne 1991), informed of advertising's 'magic system' (Williams 1980) and how globalized capitalism draws on individualism and materialism to sustain its existence.

John Perry Barlow stands out as someone who fits the bill as an archtypal construer. His work for the Electronic Frontier Foundation (www.eff.org) is as important as his contributions to the Grateful Dead. His Manifesto for Cyberspace (1991, 21) clarifies his desire to shape the technological capabilities and symbolic culture of the internet, "Consciously or unconsciously we are presently shaping the future ethics and culture of Cyberspace. Only by bringing awareness to this task will we create the sort of place we would want our children to live in". His commitment to shape the symbolic culture of the Internet has unwaivered. Barlow was interviewed as part of the BBC's Virtual Reolution project, a program that charts the emergence of cyberspace and the World Wide Web. What he said is best surmised by the Electronic Frontier Foundation's (EFF) current mission statement, centred around three fights and concerns:

> Today, certain powerful corporations are attempting to shut down online speech, prevent new innovation from reaching consumers, and facilitating government surveillance. We challenge corporate overreach just as we challenge government abuses of power.
>
> We also develop technologies that can help individuals protect their privacy and security online, which our technologists build and release freely to the public for anyone to use. In addition, EFF is engaged in major legislative fights, beating back digital censorship bills disguised as intellectual property proposals, opposing attempts to force companies to spy on users, championing reform bills that rein in government surveillance, and much more.
>
> We are working with advocates worldwide to create a global digital environment that upholds both human rights and Constitutional rights, and we continue to take on cutting-edge legal cases to win victories for user rights.

Here, Barlow and EFF engage in the building of a technological future and a symbolic culture to forge an alternative world in which the digital world is not a site of exploitation and surveillance. Yet the very thought in 2020 of a constuer consumer subject transforming all areas of social life in a short time frame cannot be treated without incredulity. Thus, the need and scope for critical marketing communications remains extensive and represents a rich opportunity for future scholarship. One aspiration for the latter is not least that it can reclaim the marketing domain's own credibility within the wider academy.

Bibliography

Andzulis, J.M., N.G. Panagopoulos, and A. Rapp (2012), "A Review of Social Media and Implications for the Sales Process," *Journal of Personal Selling & Sales Management*, 32(3), 305–16.

Bardhi, Fleura, Giana M. Eckhardt, and Eric J. Arnould (2012), "Liquid Relationship to Possessions," *Journal of Consumer Research*, 39(3), 510–29.

Barlow, J.P. (1991), "Electronic Frontier: Coming into the Country," *Communications of the ACM*, 34(3), 19–21.

Beck, Ulrich and Elisabeth Beck-Gernsheim (2002), *Individualization*, London: SAGE Publications Ltd.

Belk, Russell W. and Janeen Arnold Costa (1998), "The Mountain Man Myth: A Contemporary Consuming Fantasy," *Journal of Consumer Research*, 25(3), 218–40.

Biggs, Iain (2019), "Five Notes on Thinking Through 'Ensemble Practices,' *Climate Cultures creative conversations for the Anthropocene*, https://climatecultures.net/challenges-of-creative-engagement/five-notes-on-thinking-through-ensemble-practices/, accessed January 6, 2020.

Birdsall, Nancy and Francis Fukuyama (2011), "The Post-Washington Consensus: Development after the Crisis," *Foreign Affairs*, 90(2), 45–53.

Calthorpe, P. (1993), *The Next American Metropolis: Ecology, Community, and the American Dream*, New York: Princeton Architectural Press.

Castells, M. (2000), "Toward a Sociology of the Network Society," *Contemporary Sociology*, 29(5), 693–98.

——— (2007), "Communication, Power and Counter-Power in the Network Society," *International Journal of Communication*, 1(1), 29.

——— (2011), *The Rise of the Network Society* (Vol. 12), London: John Wiley & Sons.

Castle, T. and Lee, J. (2008), "Ordering Sex in Cyberspace: A Content Analysis of Escort Websites," *International Journal of Cultural Studies*, 11(1), 107–21.

Cova, Bernard and Daniele Dalli (2009), "Working Consumers: The Next Step in Marketing Theory?," *Marketing Theory*, 9(3), 315–39.

Crary, Jonathan (2013), *24/7: Late Capitalism and the Ends of Sleep*, London: Verso.Delphine, Dion and Eric J. Arnould (2011), "Retail Luxury Strategy: Assembling Charisma through Art and Magic," *Journal of Retailing*, 87(4), 502–20.

Donaldson, T. and P.H. Werhane, eds. (1993), *Ethical Issues in Business*, Englewood Cliffs, NJ: Prentice-Hall.

Eckhardt, G.M., R. Varman, and N. Dholakia (2019), "Ideology and Critical Marketing Studies," in *The Routledge Companion to Critical Marketing*, eds. Mark Tadajewski, Matthew Higgins, Janice Denegri-Knott, and Rohit Varman, London: Routledge, 306–18.

Ehrenfeld, D. (1978), *The Arrogance of Humanism*, New York: Oxford University Press.

Firat, A. Fuat and Alladi Venkatesh (1995), "Liberatory Postmodernism and the Reenchantment of Consumption," *The Journal of Consumer Research*, 22(3), 239–67.

Firat, A.F. and N. Dholakia (2017), "From Consumer to Construer: Travels in Human Subjectivity," *Journal of Consumer Culture*, 17(3), 504–22.

Freeland, Chrystia (2011), "The Rise of the New Global Elite," *The Atlantic*, 307(1), 44–55.

Gilbert, Jeremy (2014), *Common Ground: Democracy and Collectivity in an Age of Individualism*, London: Pluto Press.

Gimeno, J., T.B. Folta, A.C. Cooper, and C.Y. Woo (1997), "Survival of the Fittest? Entrepreneurial Human Capital and the Persistence of Underperforming Firms," *Administrative Science Quarterly*, Dec (1), 750–83.

Godelier, Maurice (2020), *The Imagined, the Imaginary and the Symbolic* (N. Scott, tran.), London: Verso.

Greene, T. William (2008), "Three Ideologies of Individualsim: Toward Assimilating a Theory of Individualisms and their Consequences," *Critical Sociology*, 34(1), 117–37.

Hirschman, E.C. (1992), "The Consciousness of Addiction: Toward a General Theory of Compulsive Consumption," *Journal of Consumer Research*, 19(2), 155–79.

——— (2003), "Men, Dogs, Guns, and Cars--The Semiotics of Rugged Individualism," *Journal of Advertising*, 32(1), 9–22.

Hobbes, T. (1950), *Leviathan*. New York: E. P. Dutton and Sons.

Hochschild, J.L. (1996), *Facing up to the American Dream: Race, Class, and the Soul of the Nation* (Vol. 51), Princeton, NJ: Princeton University Press.

Holt, Douglas B. (2002), "Why Do Brands Cause Trouble? A Dialectical Theory of Consumer Culture and Branding," *Journal of Consumer Research*, 29(1), 70–90.

——— (2004), *How Brands Become Icons: The Principles of Cultural Branding*, London: Harvard Business Press.

Holt, Douglas B. and Craig J. Thompson (2004), "Man-of-Action Heroes: The Pursuit of Heroic Masculinity in Everyday Consumption: Figure 1," *Journal of Consumer Research*, 31(2), 425–40.

Joy, Annamma, Jeff Jianfeng Wang, Tsang-Sing Chan, John F. Sherry, Jr., and Geng Cui (2014), "M(Art) Worlds: Consumer Perceptions of How Luxury Brand Stores Become Art Institutions," *Journal of Retailing*, 90(9), 347–64.

Kajonius, P.J., B.N. Persson, and P.K. Jonason (2015), "Hedonism, Achievement, and Power: Universal Values that Characterize the Dark Triad," *Personality and Individual Differences*, 77, 173–78.

Kilbourne, W.E., M.J. Dorsch, P. McDonagh, B. Urien, A. Prothero, M. Grünhagen, M. Jay Polonsky, D. Marshall, J. Foley, and A. Bradshaw (2009), "The Institutional Foundations of Materialism in Western Societies: A Conceptualization and Empirical Test," *Journal of Macromarketing*, 29(3), 259–78.

Lanchester, John (2017), "You Are the Product," *London Review of Books*, 39(16), 3–10.

Locke, J. (1963), *Two Treatises on Government*, Cambridge: Cambridge University Press.

Lukes, Steven (1971), "The Meanings of 'Individualism,' " *Journal of the History of Ideas*, 32(1), 45–66.

Macpherson, C.B. (1962), *The Political Theory of Possessive Individualism*, Oxford: The Clarendon Press.

McGuigan, Jim (2008), "Apprentices to Cool Capitalism," *Social Semiotics*, 18(3), 309–19.

Merchant, C. (1980), *The Death of Nature: Women, Ecology and the Scientific Revolution*, London: Wildwood House.

Moore, P.G. (1997), "The Development of the UK National Lottery: 1992–96," *Journal of the Royal Statistical Society: Series A (Statistics in Society)*, 160(2), 169–85.

Murray, Jeff B. and Julie L. Ozanne (1991), "The Critical Imagination: Emancipatory Interests in Consumer Research," *Journal of Consumer Research*, 18(2), 129–44.

Nietzsche, Friedrich (2006), *Thus Spoke Zarathustra*, New York: Cambridge University Press.

Shankar, Avi, Helene Cherrier, and Robin Canniford (2006), "Consumer Empowerment: A Foucauldian Interpretation," *European Journal of Marketing*, 40(9/10), 1013–30.

Sheldon, P. and K. Bryant (2016), "Instagram: Motives for Its Use and Relationship to Narcissism and Contextual Age," *Computers in Human Behavior*, 58, 89–97.

Solomon, G.T., A. Bryant, K. May, and V. Perry (2013), "Survival of the Fittest: Technical Assistance, Survival and Growth of Small Businesses and Implications for Public Policy," *Technovation*, 33(8–9), 292–301.

Srnicek, Nick and Alex Williams (2016), *Inventing the Future: Postcapitalism and a World Without Work*, London: Verso.

Streeck, Wolfgang (2017), *How Will Capitalism End? Essays on a Failing System*, London: Verso.

Thrift, Nigel (2008), *Non-representational Theory: Space, Politics, Affect*, Routledge: Abingdon.

Tocqueville, Alexis de (1835), *Democracy in America*, New York: Alfred Knopf.

Turkle, Sherry (2011), *Alone Together: Why We Expect More from Technology and Less from Each Other*, New York: Basic Books.

Virilio, Paul (1997), *Open Sky*, Verso: London.

Walter, Alexander (2017), "Amazon's Patent for 'Aquatic Storage Facilities' Could Turn Lakes into Underwater Warehouses," *Archinect*, https://archinect.com/news/article/150017459/amazon-s-patent-for-aquatic-storage-facilities-could-turn-lakes-into-underwater-warehouses, accessed January 6, 2020.

Weiwei, Ai (2019), "My Art Was Used to Sell Cars – But I'm Fighting Back," *The Guardian*, May 22, https://www.theguardian.com/commentisfree/2019/may/22/volkswagen-art-refugees-cars-ai-weiwei, accessed August 1, 2019.

Williams, Raymond (1980), "Advertising: The Magic System," *Problems in Materialism and Culture*, London: Verso, 170–95.

Zingales, L. (1998), "Survival of the Fittest or the Fattest? Exit and Financing in the Trucking Industry," *The Journal of Finance*, 53(3), 905–38.

Zwick, Detlev, Samuel K. Bonsu, and Aron Darmody (2008), "Putting Consumers to Work: 'Co-creation' and New Marketing Govern-Mentality," *Journal of Consumer Culture*, 8(2), 163–96.

Zwick, D. and A. Bradshaw (2016), "Biopolitical Marketing and Social Media Brand Communities," *Theory, Culture & Society*, 33(5), 91–115.

6

SOCIAL PROGRESS, ECONOMIC DECLINE, AND THE LOGIC OF OBJECTIVITY

Introduction

The abundance of newspaper column inches and popular literature on the subject would suggest one of the biggest challenges facing advanced capitalist societies and liberal democracies is the rise of 'fake news' (Ball 2017; D'Ancona 2017). Fake news is not objective, but it is disinformation, falsehood, and bias dressed up as fact (Tandoc, Lim, and Ling 2018). And while the *content* of fake news is deliberate lies, it mimics and takes the *form* of traditional news reporting (Waisbord 2018). This isn't to suggest that people are being duped by the visual identity of fake news websites or deceived by skilfully produced videos shared across social media. Instead, the content and form of fake news resembles the stories that are already part of political common sense (Polletta and Callahan 2017). There is little to separate the fake news intentionally produced in Macedonian teenagers' bedrooms on the run up to the 2016 US election and the reporting on some conservative mainstream media outlets (Tandoc, Lim, and Ling 2018). It is further evidence of the intensity and diffusion of post-truth that elaborate conspiracy theories aren't exclusively the preserve of oddballs, the 'weird and the wacky' (Belk 2014; Bode and Østergaard 2013), but the worldviews of those in and around the centres of economic and cultural power (Uscinski 2019) that seek to root out a fictional 'enemy within' (Goldberg 2008). Non-governmental environmental organizations were, of course, behind the fires in the Amazon in 2019 according to Brazilian President Jair Bolsonaro (Barnes 2019), and in the view of Australian senator, Concetta Fierravanti-Wells, radical 'eco-terrorists' coordinated to cause the Australian bushfires (Lagan 2020).

Fake news cannot be explained by claims that there is suddenly moral deficit at the centre of public life and that, for whatever reason, people now have few qualms about lying. Rather, fake news forms part of a much larger struggle over what counts as authoritative statements and truth claims about current events and the state of the world. Contemporary technoculture (Kozinets 2019) that combines 'infoglut' (Andrejevic 2013) and fragmentation (Firat and Venkatesh 1995) enable alternative truth claims to disseminate easily, while the term 'fake news' is uttered to dismiss and delegitimize traditional bases of authority (Tandoc, Lim, and Ling 2018) such as scientific and medical expertise (Thompson 2003, 2005). Fake news, then, is symptomatic of seismic cultural, political, and cultural transformations in relationships between public communication, epistemic and moral authority, and trust in expert systems (Davies 2018; Humphreys and Thompson 2014; Waisbord 2018). For communication scholars Farkas and Schou (2018, 302), the use of fake news as a delegitimizing utterance is emblematic of an *organic crisis* (Laclau 1990), where "the underlying symbolic systems are radically challenged and eventually recast". Yet fake news is one symptom among others that signal that historically embedded and obdurate systems of meaning and signification are being cast into doubt.

By investigating the rise and fall of once taken-for-granted measures of social progress, the purpose of this chapter is to examine another instance of these organic crises. Informed by concepts from science and technology studies, this chapter explores reasons why faith, trust, and confidence have been lost in previously 'God-like' measures such as Gross Domestic Product (GDP) and argues that objective statements about the condition of the world are in fact precarious collective achievements, whose authority stems not only from how these measures are produced but also from the social context in which their production, dissemination, and interpretation are embedded (Jasanoff 2004a). By treating facts as being 'co-produced', the breakdown of previously established self-evident 'serviceable truths' (Jasanoff and Simmet 2017) is suggestive of a transformation in the building blocks of social life, resulting in GDP becoming an unrepresentative, prejudicial, and subjective measure of social progress. We therefore explain that the loss of faith in GDP to provide an accurate representation of the state of the world is symptomatic of globalized capitalism's disintegration that benefits some people but not others. In short, what counts as truth and fact about the world is contingent upon the forms of social life and politics that people look for. Following this, we examine what alternative measures of objective social progress are currently being crafted, focusing specifically on the United Nation's (UN) *Sustainable Development Goals*. We claim that these measures constitute one way the champions of globalized capitalism have sought to reassert their authority at a time of this organic crisis, where the public have lost faith in traditional measures to know, assess, and represent social progress.

Knowing the unknowable

No one has direct access to reality, so what is the state of the world? How can we make the 'social totality' (Jameson 1992) comprehensible and intelligible? How do we know the world is improving or declining? What element of the world should be rendered visible and the focus of attention?

Market-based societies have developed their own 'regime of perceptibility' (Crary 2001), which, for Slater and Tonkiss (2001, 26), is based on "three components: labour, commodification, and monetarization and calculation". The emergence of these three components allows an abstract thing called 'the economy' to come into being (Hirschman 2016). As a result of the calculation and quantification, on the one hand, and ideas about what counts as social progress, on the other, market-based societies have developed number-based measures of tracking and understand social progress. Specifically, social progress is not expressed through more emic, involved, and qualitative measures of progress such as community cohesiveness (Bouchet 2018) but through number-based figures that are premised on being able to represent the world without prejudice or subjective judgement. This necessarily involves distance and detachment, a "disenchantment of the world" (Slater and Tonkiss 2001, 75) via forms of technical expertise and calculative practices whose authority stems from their purported objectivity (Power 2004, 2011).

"Objectivity", Gaukroger (2001, 10785) writes,

> stands in contrast to subjectivity: an objective account is one which attempts to capture the nature of the object studied in a way that does not depend on any features of the particular subject who studies it. An objective account is, in this sense, impartial, one which could ideally be accepted by any subject, because it does not draw on any assumptions, prejudices, or values of particular subjects.

Objective knowledge paints a picture of the social whole with a "conquering gaze from nowhere" (Haraway 1988, 581). Accordingly, things that are granted the status of being 'objective' are removed from the realm of public debate, since 'being objective' is impersonal and disinterested, and exists independent of the people and instruments that help form it (Latour 1999; Shore and Wright 2015); objective things are things as they actually are.

GDP as measure of social progress

For the majority of the 20th century, GDP formed the objective measure to track social progress (Davies 2018). First developed for the US Congress in 1934, GDP, or Gross National Income, became the principal measure of and social progress through the combination of statistical advancement, the convergence of previously disparate economic thought, and, most crucially, the impact of the Great Depression on the US Government, since this social and economic disruption sensitized politicians to the need to measure *economic* outcomes to understand *social* development (Hirschman 2016). GDP measures the market value of all goods and services produced in a specific time period, typically a year. A quick search for 'What is the importance of measuring per capita GDP?' reports the following,

> *GDP per capita is a measure of a country's economic output* that accounts for its number of people. It divides the country's gross domestic product by its total population. *That makes it the best measurement of a country's standard of living. It tells you how prosperous a country feels to each of its citizens.*

While it is important to emphasize the critical limitations of GDP in terms of what it misses out (Hochschild 1989), it is also as crucial to not dismiss its importance because in doing so we would overlook how GDP figures remain integral to 'technologies of government' (see Miller and Rose 2009; Rose 1991, 2000), which continue to bestow political actors with legitimacy and authority. As a national measure, it permits governments to determine and make claims about how well the economy is performing, and is a device deployed to make some sort of judgement about the fundamental health of a society. As the recent examples of India and America show, GDP is to authoritarian 'strong men' leaders (see Gusterson 2017; Lamont, Park, and Ayala-Hurtado 2017; Robin 2017), as the 'Dodgy Dossier' was to Alistair Campbell and Tony Blair, an invaluable device to retain some degree of authority. Despite Donald Trump's ideological incoherence (Riley 2018), GDP is one thing that he is nevertheless obsessed with (Mitra 2018). And while it is impossible to say that his preoccupation with it stems from its status as a proxy for social progress, GDP's standing as an invaluable heuristic stems from, as Haworth (1977, 4) explains, its ability to paint a picture of economic and social life,

> Capitalism is justified as an effective manner of organizing economic life so that we may be assured a high and increasing G[DP]. Except among fanatics, a high G[DP] is not valued for itself but for the number of jobs and the level of consumption it underwrites.

GDP's demise

As we intimated in Chapter 2, GDP has lost its lustre. Apart from its most impassioned defenders, no longer do people have faith in GDP to represent the health of the country, nor the quality of life of those people living in it. This lack of faith, trust, and confidence in GDP as an accurate measure of social progress is not a perspective held by Internet cranks who treat it as an expression of 'fifth filter' propaganda that is subject to government and political manipulation (Schiff 2013) but the view held by representatives of the business press (Dawkins 2019). Consider the following, by Gilliant Tett (2019), writing in the *Financial Times* under the title 'To GDP or not to GDP?'

Next week the US government releases its latest data on gross domestic product for the third quarter of 2019. It's a fair bet that this will trigger debate among pundits in Washington and on Wall Street about whether the world's largest economy is heading for a recession — and what that might mean for the re-election of Donald Trump. *But, as investors scrutinise those seemingly precise digits, are we missing a trick? Is it possible that apparently crucial GDP numbers are actually an illusion — or a distortion — when it comes to assessing the economy?* That is the seemingly heretical idea currently being tossed around some parts of America's Federal Reserve, as well as in academia and parts of Wall Street. For as Silicon Valley keeps delivering new technological innovations, these are not only transforming how we live but also overall growth. Some economists fear, therefore, that our old measures of GDP no longer capture the "real" economy, not just in terms of output but also of prices and our own incomes.

Some of these statements would not be out of place on a paranoid YouTube channel that tries to peddle hoax cures, survivalist equipment, while rallying against the 'globalist' elite (Uscinski 2019). That this degree of doubt is cast upon GDP's usefulness as a measure to capture the 'social totality' (Jameson 1992) indicates that GDP has lost its authority, and that it is treated as a measure that can be concocted out of thin air, bearing no relation to the actual state of the world.

We submit that the demise of GDP is part and parcel of a much broader malaise and disenchantment with the project of globalized capitalism. Wolfgang Streeck (2017, 242–43), for instance, reminds us here that "many today feel that the current financial and fiscal crisis is not just an economic but fundamentally a social matter important enough to demand a revised interpretation of modern society". There is then a pervasive feeling that measures such as GDP are unable to capture the true reality of the economy, and that statements and proclamations about the growth of the economy are treated with the same level of scepticism and bemusements that met statements about the reasons for entering Iraq in 2003. But why, specifically, have people lost faith in GDP as a reliable measure of social progress?

To answer this question, we turn to ideas in science and technology studies and the concept of co-production (Haraway 1988; Jasanoff 2004a) to explain that what counts as truth and fact about the world is never objective, but rather is contingent upon the forms of politics that people desire and look for, produced in moments of a society's instrumental, aesthetic, and epistemological strivings. In view of this explanation, we then examine the rampant inequality that pervades many advanced capitalist societies and suggest that the disconnect between, on the one hand, the claim that GDP is increasing and social life is improving and, on the other hand, lived 'near-at-hand' (Geertz 1973, 1974) reality means that people find it difficult to place trust in previously dominant measures of social progress.

The co-production of objective social facts

In recent decades, the field of science and technologies studies has gone some way to illuminate the relationship between politics, society, and knowledge production (Haraway 1988; Latour 1999; Latour and Woolgar 1979). One of the field's key sensitizing concepts is that of co-production (Jasanoff 2004a), the "proposition that the ways in which we know and represent the world are inseparable from the ways in which we choose to live in it" (Jasanoff 2004b, 2). 'Objective' social facts about the world we live in are therefore not transcendent, 'purified' (Canniford and Shankar 2013; Latour 1993) mirrors of reality but are instead embedded, formed, and cast in the social. By working on the basis that objective social facts are contingent upon the social, the concept of co-production has been criticized for casting doubt on the belief that knowledge production and 'science' is value free, undermining systems of expertise (Giddens 1990), let alone the idea that there exists an independent reality, unblemished by human action and bias that can be accessed, studied, and understood through science (Dalston and Galison 2010; Latour 1999). Far from denying an independent reality, however, co-production stresses how such beliefs rest on Enlightenment discourses and, as a result, draws attention to the social dimensions of science. The benefit of treating the social as being indissolubly tied up to the way knowledge is produced, represented, and received is that it enables us to treat knowledge not as separate to culture, politics, and economies but instead as intertwined. From this co-production perspective, knowledge and fact's capacity to offer a legitimate representation of reality can weaken should people's lived realities, social practices, and ideologies shift.

It is therefore little wonder why GDP lost its shine, given that it is no longer able to reflect the lived economic and social experience of large swaths of American and British populations. William Davies provides a window into how GDP becomes a useless measure in times of inequality, when economic improvements are not distributed equally but favour the already well off. As Davies (2018, 76) explains,

> Indicators such as GDP capture things in the aggregate, while GDP per capita captures what this means for people on average. But the divisive effect of economic inequality is such that aggregates and averages are simply no longer credible representations of how things are.

With economic improvements being distributed unequally across the very countries that championed globalized capitalism, there is little wonder that rallying calls behind GDP growth and increases in the stock market fail to resonate with vast swathes of the population. While objective measures of social progress may resonate in social circumstances where there are equal gains being made by all sections of society, they nevertheless fail to speak to people's lived experiences as advanced capitalist economies continue down the path of declining growth, accelerating distributional conflict, and the intensification of inequality that stems from this (Alvaredo et al. 2017; Streeck 2017).

Progress at a time of crisis

Just as we are living in a political and social *interregnum* where it is unclear what exactly will replace globalized capitalism, we are living through a numerical period of indeterminacy. How should we measure social progress? Whatever measure politicians and economists settle on, it will be one that represents and speaks to the dominant ideology of that time and the interests of those at the centre of economic, social, and cultural power than those at the margins.

There are lessons to be learnt from management here. For corporations, the measure of progress and success has historically been the profit line (Williams and Williams 2010), as management has used it to please, satisfy, and placate investors such as banking and shareholders. However, measures of progress in the business world have proliferated due to the avalanche of key performance indicators, which can be used to mask and hide poor performance. Consider, for instance, the way in which WeWork's messianic CEO was able to hide eye-watering losses and lack of profitable business plan for years, yet had been able to maintain credibility through a combination of charisma, charm, and 'sunny projections' (Zeitlin 2019).

An 'avalanche of numbers', to borrow Ian Hacking's (1982) phrase, while allowing abstraction and the mapping of social progress simultaneously enables obfuscation (Espeland and Sauder 2016). This isn't exactly novel; the crisis in marketing's use resulted in the proliferation of 'marketing metrics', ranging from sales and leads generated, website traffic generated, click-throughs per day (Greenfield 2017), to the extent of media coverage. Such measures are used as rhetorical devices to maintain credibility and used to maintain access to resources, and ultimately provide sources of legitimation (Humphreys 2010) that sustain a business at a time of uncertain financial certainty. If you consider any of the *IPA Advertising Effectiveness Awards*, you will find this trope commonly played out.

Consider Audi, Gold Award case winner in 2018, with its account of "Beauty and brains: How we supercharged the Audi premium 2015–2018", which won praise for its return on marketing investment (ROMI) run by the BBH agency:

> Audi's UK growth had come from its less expensive cars. It aspired to sell more cars to higher value customers. Using a strategic idea of the 'progressive premium', Audi launched a programme to communicate the desirability and technical innovation of its cars to higher spending users across various channels. Following the activity, Audi became top for desirability among the prestige audience. Sales volumes grew three times faster than the UK market. Between 2015 and 2017, an estimated £1.78bn of incremental revenue was generated and the profit ROMI was £2.07 for every £1 invested.

Who could argue with such logic that a successful business knows 'what it is doing if it can produce hard evidence' of effective returns on investment? Another example reinforcing this logic comes from the 'Business to Business category' of the Public Relations (PR) Awards, announced 16 October 2018 by PRWeek, where the winner of the year's best Business-to-Business (B2B) campaign award was Frank. The agency's 'Populating Plexal – The AI legacy of London 2012' helped client Plexal achieve a target-smashing launch. Frank was given a brief to encourage enquiries, registration, and occupancy for Plexal. Plexal is an 'ideas hub' for tech businesses housed in the former London 2012 Olympics Broadcast Centre. This has become a key part of the Olympics legacy plan. Plexal was a building site when Frank took on the brief. At that time, there was a lack of assets, even a computer-generated image, for the media. So, the main 'asset' became Plexal's chief executive Claire Cockerton, who was promoted by the agency to key titles as a 'commentator on all things' tech-related. The results were summarized as follows:

> Highlights included featuring in *The Times* on the day of the Spring Budget Statement, becoming a regular guest on the BBC Radio 4 *Today* programme, and being quoted by *The Daily Telegraph*, *New Statesman* and The Independent.
>
> The activity generated more than 100 pieces of coverage from day one to 'doors open', when occupancy rates were 60 per cent, against a target of 35 per cent. Ninety per cent of initial occupants were from Plexal's desired sector of robotics and AI (the target was 70 per cent). PR was the sole marketing function that led to enquiries, tour registrations and long-term occupancy agreements.
>
> The Mayor of London's office asked Plexal to be part of the #LondonIsOpen campaign to reinforce London as a tech hub post-Brexit, and the Mayor launched London Tech Week at Plexal's opening.

For many businesses, objective reality is a matter of quantification and producing a world of numbers (Hacking 1982; Power 2004). This is because simple numbers "require less interpretive work than [more complex] composites and are less vulnerable to the twists produced by long interpretive chains" (Merry 2016, 217). Numbers make decision-making easier. It removes subjective judgement and local knowledge from the situation (Geertz 1973). Numbers remain powerful "strategies of communication" (Porter 1995, viii) that resonate with the business world, regardless of their content, context, or, indeed, the relation of they have the real world.

Potential future measures of social progress

Objective social measures of progress such as GDP remain useful when they speak to a shared reality (Jasanoff 2004a). When indeterminacy reins, objective measures of social progress require reinvigoration (Roche, O'Connell, and Prothero 2016). For many reasons, not least the GFC based on the global contagion of the drying up of interbank lending, there is greater uncertainty about how social progress can be measured. For a time, happiness led the field for becoming the 'God-like' measure to replace GDP to assess social progress. Frawley (2015, 62) notes that the happiness 'turn' (Davies 2015; Merry 2016) received a real boost when,

> following appointment as President of the American Psychological Associ-
> ation in 1998, Martin Seligman outlined plans for a 'new science of human
> strengths', termed 'positive psychology'. The new sub-discipline would
> aim to be a 'science of positive subjective experience, positive individual
> traits, and positive institutions,' seeking to 'improve quality of life and pre-
> vent pathologies that arise when life is barren and meaningless' (Seligman
> and Csikszentmihalyi 2000:5). Since its creation in the late 1990s, Ruut
> Veenhoven's multi-disciplinary *World Database of Happiness* has grown to
> include nearly 7000 studies, many relying on self-report questionnaires
> (Veenhoven 2014; see also Rusk and Waters 2013). It is claimed that hap-
> piness is measurable and represents serious 'hard' science differing from
> traditional self-help for its commitment to empiricism.
>
> *(Diener 2000; Layard 2011; Lyubomirsky 2007; Nettle 2005)*

That the *World Happiness Report* is in the seventh edition demonstrates how suc-
cessful the 'well-being' movement has been in institutionalizing their values. However, it is environment and ecological concerns *en masse* which have led many to rally behind a measure of social progress that seeks to build tentative and continuous compromises between planet, people, and profit (Belz and Pe-
attie 2012). In Chapter 4 on sustainability, we consider in greater depth the way in which management has placated systemic critique of globalized capitalism's systemic tendency towards ecological destruction through the idea of corporate social responsibility. However, in view of the co-production of social facts and the parallelism between knowledge production and politics, then it is no surprise that businesses have been invited to help develop a vision of future social progress.

The UN's Sustainable Development Goals offer a long-term future for 2030 based on 17 difference measures to determine a consensually agreed understand-
ing of social progress (Griggs et al. 2013; Robert, Parris, and Leiserowitz 2005; Salvia et al. 2019). While these goals on paper call for systemic transformation in every country that agreed to them, demanding the combined efforts of governments, business, science, and civil society to succeed, critics have pointed to the lack of formal and informal mechanisms to ensure that nation states and the busi-
ness that operate in them adhere to them (Sachs et al. 2019). Although good on paper, there is little in the way of ideas, policy, or practice that emphasizes how these goals should be implemented, nor how the UN can force countries to take them seriously. Nevertheless, by signing up to development goals, politicians of various stripes place themselves in a position of credibility and legitimacy.

Beck and Levy (2013, 13–14) write about the unbundling of nationhood through global capital. They submit that transnational production processes and the very transnational institutions of commercial law constitute a major transformation of active self-cosmopolitanization of the nation state. This transformation echoes what McDonagh, Kilbourne, and Prothero (2014) have reminded us is the prevailing order. It would seem that deregulation is a vehicle through which states are incorporating the world market regime. In this way, states appear to be guaranteeing the rights of global capital as an essential ingredient of the national. This *naturalization* of global capital occurs at length and no matter what the crisis business seems to be able to continue as usual, impervious to any call for concession and change; they remark,

> "No one can do politics against the markets." Joschka Fischer's dictum is emblematic of the self-image of the political class over the past two decades. Politicians see themselves as pawns in a power game dominated by globally operating capital. Here we are dealing with a self-delusion of unpolitical innocence in a twofold sense: on the one hand, it glosses over the fact that the political class brought about the alleged powerlessness to act through its own conduct. Specifically, it imposed the rules of the globalized markets at the national level under the banner of "reform policy", thus giving rise to the allegedly no longer controllable financial world risk capitalism. Note that global capital acquires its "unchallengeable" power only when national politics actively colludes in its own self-abolition (Beck 2012). On the other hand, the self-inflicted impotence of politics serves as a convenient excuse to deflect the pressure to act within global domestic politics and not to make use of the opportunities for action that are opening up. Since there are no consensual global political answers to the consequences of globalization, *allegedly nothing can be done!*

It is against such radical pessimism that we submit the tools of critical marketing communications can help people decipher how 'objective social progress' lives a parallel life to politics. It isn't uncommon for marketing communications and advertising to appropriate and co-opt social trends (Frank and Weiland 1997; Holt 2002, 2004; Holt and Cameron 2010; McDonagh and Brereton 2010). Opinion pieces at the start of the last decade by attorneys at law Devika Kewalramani (partner and co-chair of Moses & Singer LLP's Legal Ethics & Law Firm Practice group) and Richard J. Sobelsohn (attorney in Moses & Singer's Real Estate practice and a LEED® Accredited Professional) and curated by Roy (2012) in the hallowed ground of *Forbes* magazine warned of the tightrope that corporations were treading and the legal repercussions of errors,

> As more businesses jump on the green bandwagon, and rising public intolerance for false green claims is experienced, it is only a matter of time before there is a groundswell in court actions or other proceedings.

Sheehan and Morrison (2018) challenge advertising leaders to step up to the climate change emergency, and Fleischman (2014) encourages people to look beyond the illusions of headlines to see what is going on. Writing for *Campaign* Steven Bennett-Day (2019), founder of Few & Far, mulls over the PR benefits for any agency in partnering with the activist group Extinction Rebellion, he underscores the basic point nicely when he opines,

> This industry needs a lesson in how to actually do something "good". It's very fashionable to talk about or appear to be doing your bit. Many agencies are working to become B Corp-certified and adland has even held its own climate summit. But if you aren't doing anything tangible to help reverse climate change, improve sustainability or reduce your and your clients' impact, all you're doing is engaging in a load of greenwashing.

As such, until we see material and tangible concessions from business, we suggest that green initiatives formed through alliances between the business elite and transnational organizations should be met with some degree of initial legal as well as consumer scepticism.

Bibliography

Alvaredo, Facundo, Lucas Chancel, Thomas Piketty, Emmanuel Saez, and Gabriel Zucman (2017), "Global Inequality Dynamics: New Findings from WID.world," *American Economic Review*, 107(5), 404–9.

Andrejevic, Mark (2013), *Infoglut: How Too Much Information is Changing the Way We Think and Know*, New York: Routledge.

Ball, James (2017), *Post-Truth: How Bullshit Conquered the World*, London: Biteback.

Barnes, Luke (2019), "Bolsonaro's Conspiracy Theories Are Making Brazil's Rainforest Wildfires Worse," *The National Interest*, Text, The Center for the National Interest, https://nationalinterest.org/blog/buzz/bolsonaros-conspiracy-theories-are-making-brazils-rainforest-wildfires-worse-75441, accessed March 28, 2020.

Beck, Ulrich and Daniel Levy (2013), "Cosmopolitanized Nations: Re-imaginging Collectivity in World Risk Society," *Theory, Culture and Society*, 30(2), 3–31.

Belk, Russell (2014), "The Labors of the Odysseans and the Legacy of the Odyssey," *Journal of Historical Research in Marketing*, (P. Mark Tadajewski, ed.), 6(3), 379–404.

Belz, Frank-Martin and Ken Peattie (2012), *Sustainability Marketing: A Global Perspective*, London: Wiley.

Bode, Matthias and Per Østergaard (2013), "'The Wild and Wacky Worlds of Consumer Oddballs': Analyzing the Manifestary Context of Consumer Culture Theory," *Marketing Theory*, 13(2), 175–92.

Bouchet, Dominque (2018), "Marketing, Violence and Social Cohesion: First Steps to a Conceptual Approach to the Understanding of the Normalising Role of Marketing," *Journal of Marketing Management*, 34(11–12), 1048–62.

Canniford, Robin and Avi Shankar (2013), "Purifying Practices: How Consumers Assemble Romantic Experiences of Nature," *Journal of Consumer Research*, 39(5), 1051–69.

Crary, Jonathan (2001), *Suspensions of Perception: Attention, Spectacle, and Modern Culture*, Boston, MA: Massacheusetts Institute of Technology.

Dalston, Lorraine and Peter Galison (2010), *Objectivity*, Brooklyn, NY: Zone Books.

D'Ancona, Matthew (2017), *Post Truth: The New War on Truth and How to Fight Back*, London: Ebury.

Davies, William (2015), *The Happiness Industry: How the Big Government and Big Business Sold us Well-Being*, London: Verso.

———— (2018), *Nervous States: How Feeling Took Over the World*, London: Jonathan Cape.

Dawkins, David (2019), "GDP Is Broken – Meet The Leaders Trying To Fix It," *Forbes*, https://www.forbes.com/sites/daviddawkins/2019/08/03/gdp-is-brokenmeet-the-leaders-trying-to-fix-it/, accessed January 7, 2020.

Espeland, Wendy and Michael Sauder (2016), *Engines of Anxiety: Academic Rankings, Reputation, and Accountability*, London: Russel Sage Foundation.

Farkas, Johan and Jannick Schou (2018), "Fake News as a Floating Signifier: Hegemony, Antagonism and the Politics of Falsehood," *Javnost – The Public*, 25(3), 298–314.

Firat, A. Fuat and Alladi Venkatesh (1995), "Liberatory Postmodernism and the Reenchantment of Consumption," *The Journal of Consumer Research*, 22(3), 239–67.

Frank, Thomas and Matt Weiland (1997), *Commodify Your Dissent: Salvos from the Baffler*, New York: W.W. Norton.

Frawley, Ashley (2015), "Happiness Research: A Review of Critiques," *Sociology Compass*, 9(1), 62–77.

Gaukroger, Stephen (2001), "Objectivity, History of," in *International Encyclopedia of the Social and Behavioural Sciences, 26 vols.*, eds. N.J. Smelser and P.B. Baltes, New York: Amsterdam, 10785–89.

Geertz, Clifford (1973), *The Interpretation of Cultures*, New York: Basic Books.

———— (1974), "'From the Native's Point of View': On the Nature of Anthropological Understanding," *Bulletin of the American Academy of Arts and Sciences*, 28(1), 26–45.

Giddens, Anthony (1990), *The Consequences of Modernity*, Cambridge: Polity Press.

Goldberg, Robert Alan (2008), *Enemies Within: The Culture of Conspiracy in Modern America*, New Haven, CT: Yale University Press.

Greenfield, Adam (2017), *Radical Technologies: The Design of Everyday Life*, London: Verso.

Griggs, David, Mark Stafford-Smith, Owen Gaffney, Johan Rockström, Marcus C. Öhman, Priya Shyamsundar, Will Steffen, Gisbert Glaser, Norichika Kanie, and Ian Noble (2013), "Sustainable Development Goals for People and Planet," *Nature*, 495(7441), 305–7.

Gusterson, Hugh (2017), "From Brexit to Trump: Anthropology and the Rise of Nationalist Populism: From Brexit to Trump," *American Ethnologist*, 44(2), 209–14.

Hacking, Ian (1982), "Biopower and the Avalanche of Printed Numbers," *Humanities in Society*, 5(3–4), 279–95.

Haraway, Donna (1988), "Situated Knowledges: The Science Question in Feminism and the Privilege of Partial Perspective," *Feminist Studies*, 14(3), 575–99.

Haworth, Lawrence (1977), *Decadence and Objectivity: Ideals for Work in the Post-Consumer Society*, Toronto: University of Toronto Press.

Hirschman, Daniel Abramson (2016), "Inventing the Economy Or: How We Learned to Stop Worrying and Love the GDP," Unpublished PhD Dissertation: University of Michigan.

Hochschild, Arlie Russell (1989), *The Second Shift*, London: Penguin Books.

Holt, Douglas B. (2002), "Why Do Brands Cause Trouble? A Dialectical Theory of Consumer Culture and Branding," *Journal of Consumer Research*, 29(1), 70–90.

———— (2004), *How Brands Become Icons: The Principles of Cultural Branding*, London: Harvard Business Press.

Holt, Douglas B. and Douglas Cameron (2010), *Cultural Strategy: Using Innovative Ideologies to Build Breakthrough Brands*, Oxford: Oxford University Press.

Humphreys, Ashlee (2010), "Megamarketing: The Creation of Markets as a Social Process," *Journal of Marketing*, 74(2), 1–19.

Humphreys, Ashlee and Craig J. Thompson (2014), "Branding Disaster: Reestablishing Trust through the Ideological Containment of Systemic Risk Anxieties," *Journal of Consumer Research*, 41(4), 877–910.

Jameson, Fredric (1992), *Postmodernism: Or, the Cultural Logic of Late Capitalism*, New York: Verso.

Jasanoff, Sheila, ed. (2004a), *States of Knowledge: The Co-Production of Science and Social Order*, London: Routledge.

——— (2004b), "The Idiom of Co-production," in *States of Knowledge: The Co-production of Science and Social Order*, ed. S. Jasanoff, London: Routledge, 1–12.

Jasanoff, Sheila and Hilton R. Simmet (2017), "No Funeral Bells: Public Reason in a 'Post-Truth' Age," *Social Studies of Science*, 47(5), 751–70.

Kozinets, Robert V. (2019), "Consuming Technocultures: An Extended JCR Curation," *Journal of Consumer Research*, 46(3), 620–27.

Laclau, Ernesto (1990), *New Reflections on the Revolution of Our Times*, London: Verso.

Lagan, Bernard (2020), "Eco-Terrorist Group Started Australia's Devastating Bushfires, Senator Claims," *The Times*, https://www.thetimes.co.uk/article/sinister-eco-terrorists-may-have-started-australias-devastating-bushfires-senator-claims-npk2psb6v, accessed January 6, 2020.

Lamont, Michèle, Bo Yun Park, and Elena Ayala-Hurtado (2017), "Trump's Electoral Speeches and His Appeal to the American White Working Class," *British Journal of Sociology*, 68(1), 153–80.

Latour, Bruno (1993), *We Have Never Been Modern*, Harvard University Press.

——— (1999), *Pandora's Hope: Essays on the Reality of Science Study*, New York: Harvard University Press.

Latour, Bruno and Steve Woolgar (1979), *Laboratory Life: The Construction of Scientific Facts*, Princeton University Press.

McDonagh, Pierre and P. Brereton (2010), "Screening Not Greening: An Ecological Reading of the Greatest Business Movies," *Journal of Macromarketing*, 30(2), 133–46.

McDonagh, P., W.E. Kilbourne, and A. Prothero (2014), "Re-affirming the Prevailing Order?," in *Humanistic Marketing*, ed. Richard J. Varey and Michael Pirson, Palgrave Macmillan, London, 29–38.

Merry, Sally Engle (2016), *The Seductions of Quantification: Measuring Human Rights, Gender Violence, and Sex Trafficking*, The University of Chicago Press.

Miller, Peter and Nikolas S. Rose (2009), *Governing the Present: Administering Economic, Social and Personal Life*, Cambridge: Polity Press.

Mitra, Sophie (2018), "The US Needs to get over its Obsession with GDP," *The Conversation*, http://theconversation.com/the-us-needs-to-get-over-its-obsession-with-gdp-101065, accessed March 30, 2020.

Polletta, Francesca and Jessica Callahan (2017), "Deep Stories, Nostalgia Narratives, and Fake News: Storytelling in the Trump Era," *American Journal of Cultural Sociology*, 5(3), 392–408.

Porter, Theodore M. (1995), *Trust in Numbers: The Pursuit of Objectivity in Science and Public Life*, Princeton University Press.

Power, Michael (2004), "Counting, Control and Calculation: Reflectons on Measuring and Management," *Human Relations*, 57(6), 765–83.

——— (2011), "Foucault and Sociology," *Annual Review of Sociology*, 37(1), 35–56.

Riley, Dylan (2018), "What is Trump?," *New Left Review*, 114(Nov–Dec), 5–31.

Robert, Kates W., Thomas M. Parris, and Anthony A. Leiserowitz (2005), "What is Sustainable Development? Goals, Indicators, Values, and Practice," *Environment: Science and Policy for Sustainable Development*, 47(3), 8–21.

Robin, Corey (2017), *The Reactionary Mind: Conservatism from Edmund Burke to Donald Trump*, Oxford University Press.

Roche, William K., Philip O'Connell, and Andrea Prothero, eds. (2016), *Austerity and Recovery in Ireland: Europe's Poster Child and the Great Recession*, Oxford University Press.

Rose, Nikolas (1991), "Governing by Numbers: Figuring out Democracy," *Accounting, Organizations and Society*, 16(7), 673–92.

——— (2000), "Government and Control," *The British Journal of Criminology*, 40(2), 321–39.

Sachs, Jeffrey D., Guido Schmidt-Traub, Mariana Mazzucato, Dirk Messner, Nebojsa Nakicenovic, and Johan Rockstrom (2019), "Six Transformations to Achieve the Sustainable Development Goals," *Nature Sustainability*, 2, 805–14.

Salvia, Amanda Lange, Walter Leal Filho, Luciana Londero Brandli, and Juliane Sapper Griebeler (2019), "Assessing Research Trends Related to Sustainable Development Goals: Local and Global Issues," *Journal of Cleaner Production*, 208, 841–49.

Schiff, Peter (2013), *GDP Propaganda Exposed*, https://www.youtube.com/watch?v=g5O fBxk00LI, accessed January 7, 2020.

Shore, Cris and Susan Wright (2015), "Governing by Numbers: Audit Culture, Rankings and the New World Order: GOVERNING BY NUMBERS," *Social Anthropology*, 23(1), 22–28.

Streeck, Wolfgang (2017), *How Will Capitalism End? Essays on a Failing System*, London: Verso.

Tandoc, Edson C., Zheng Wei Lim, and Richard Ling (2018), "Defining 'Fake News': A Typology of Scholarly Definitions," *Digital Journalism*, 6(2), 137–53.

Tett, Gillian (2019), "To GDP — or not to GDP?," *Financial Times*, https://www.ft.com/content/cec57b2e-f522-11e9-a79c-bc9acae3b654, accessed January 7, 2020.

Thompson, Craig J. (2003), "Natural Health Discourses and the Therapeutic Production of Consumer Resistance," *The Sociological Quarterly*, 44(1), 81–107.

——— (2005), "Consumer Risk Perceptions in a Community of Reflexive Doubt," *Journal of Consumer Research*, 32 (2), 235–48.

Uscinski, Joseph E., ed. (2019), *Conspiracy Theories and the People Who Believe Them*, Oxford, New York: Oxford University Press.

Waisbord, Silvio (2018), "Truth is What Happens to News: On Journalism, Fake News, and Post-truth," *Journalism Studies*, 19(3), 1866–78.

Williams, S. and N. Williams (2010), *The Profit Impact of Business Intelligence*, London: Elsevier.

Zeitlin, Matthew (2019), "Why WeWork Went Wrong," *The Guardian*, https://www.theguardian.com/business/2019/dec/20/why-wework-went-wrong, accessed January 7, 2020.

7

BOREDOM

Digitized '24/7' connectivity and the logic of distraction

Introduction

It has been nearly 40 years since marketing and consumer researchers first proposed that an analysis of the hedonic, aesthetic, and emotional aspects of consumption might explain why people buy what they buy and do what they do (Holbrook and Hirschman 1982). They were right to observe that post Second World War consumer culture promised an abundance of pleasure, fun, and escape in the Fordist era of dull, dreary, and repetitive work (Lasch 1979; Lears 1983). During this period, advertising had the knack of appropriating beautiful imagery, people, sounds, and music to render the most mundane and workaday of activities exciting, entertaining, and transformative.

Shaving company Gillette's long-running ad campaign with the tagline 'the best a man can get' is one example where advertising's reputation as a magic system (Williams 1980) is on full display, turning a simple tool that cuts hair into an object central to invented rituals of self-transformation. With its extensive use of images, people, and sounds, Gillette's advertising turns shaving into a ritual through which tousled, unkempt 'lumbersexuals' turn into upstanding young men of self-respect (Martin 1995). Such timeless campaigns remind us once again of Williamson's (1978, 45) analysis that advertisements exist to conceal, mask, and distort the true nature of everyday life by providing consumers a 're-hash of mythological elements' and playful identities to live through.

For critical theorists, the only sensible prognosis here is that marketing communications is in the business of manufacturing diversions, distractions, and amusements that allow people to 'take flight' and escape from the oppressive reality of their lives (Held 1990; Horkheimer and Adorno 1996). The desire for distraction stems from the drudgery, responsibility, and strains of everyday life and the 'sameness' of existence produced under globalized capitalism. What else could explain why consumers seek out 'extraordinary' experiences other than compensation for the ruinous effects of urbanized life, labour, and an endless stream of numbing entertainment (Canniford and Shankar 2013; Scott, Cayla, and Cova 2017)? That these experiences also prevent political thought and action from emerging is just a welcomed addition.

The aim of this chapter is not to add to our understanding that extraordinary, hedonistic experiences provide temporary, restorative relief from the workaday oppression of everyday life. In contrast, this chapter argues that globalized capitalism's world of intensive, on-demand service, information overload, and compulsory digital '24/7' connectivity (Crary 2013; Husemann and Eckhardt 2019) result in a new form of distraction centred around *boredom*, an affective state of disengaged absorption (Anderson 2004). Specifically, this chapter sketches out how the abundance of on-demand service and compulsory digital connectivity of globalized capitalism precludes the possibility of 'profound boredom' (Heidegger 1995) by providing consumers with an endless stream of low-level stimuli for the purpose of constant distraction. We conclude that boredom is the affective state that best correlates with the accelerated connectivity which digital capitalism has ushered in.

Distraction as hedonic, absorbed escape

Marketing and consumer researchers have traditionally conceived distraction as being sourced through hedonic consumer experiences that provide temporary release from the workaday drudgery of contemporary life. This is the basis of the experience economy (Pine and Gilmore 2011) in which 'escape attempts' (Taylor and Cohen 1976) provide essential 'safety valves' through which consumers can return to ordinary life renewed, refreshed, and reinvigorated. This section examines four categories of hedonic escape to demonstrate how underpinning each is high levels of consumer absorption and involvement, *fun, fantasy, fragility and fitness*, and *festival*. By introducing these instances of traditional forms of distraction, we then pose the question: what if these examples overlook how distraction is being configured differently in this era of globalized capitalism?

Fun. Marketing and consumer research explains how forms of escape have been successfully orchestrated through the facilitation of play (O'Sullivan and Shankar 2019; Seregina and Weijo 2016), activities that are as captivating and absorbing as they are unserious and inconsequential. "Play", Caillois (1950, 212) writes, "rests, distracts, and causes the dangers, cares, and travails of life to be forgotten". Although marketing and consumer research witnesses play in social movements (Weijo, Martin, and Arnould 2018), it is consumer tribes that exhibit most clearly the capacity to use play to create something that is *new*, or what did not exist earlier (Roffe 2020). Despite their transience, tribes engage in 'active play' (Cova, Kozinets, and Shankar 2007) through which cultural, material, and emotional resources are played with, reconfigured, and reassembled in new combinations (Canniford 2011; Hargadon 2003). Despite the personal restorative benefits active play provides consumers, it is important not to overlook how the fruits of consumer play often form sources of value for brands (Mamali, Nuttall, and Shankar 2018; Molesworth and Janice 2008; O'Sullivan and Shankar 2019). Indeed, the affective, playful outcomes of tribes are just among similar versions of consumer-centred value production in which consumers remain happy while being exploited, unwaged, and milked for their creative capacities (Cova and Dalli 2009; Thrift 2008).

Fantasy. These transient instances of active play can, however, become more sustained in consumer's leisure time, animated by past-oriented or future-oriented visions of an alternative lifeworld. Whether it is cosplay (Kozinets 2001; Seregina and Weijo 2016), LARPs (Orazi and Cruz 2019; Seregina 2018), or historical re-enactments and cultural performances (Belk and Costa 1998; Peñaloza 2001), the formation of these fantasy worlds has been chronicled by marketing and consumer researchers, who have drawn attention to how consumers' "indulgence in the hallucinatory realization of desires" (Žižek 1997, 13) is formed through shared experiences and the appropriation of a mythic past or future imaginary (Belk and Costa 1998; Kozinets 2001; Seregina 2018; Seregina and Weijo 2016). These performed fantasy worlds do not just engender an 'imagined community' of like-minded people (Muñiz and O'Guinn 2001; Muñiz and Schau 2005) but produce instead an embodied community who work to carve out idiosyncratic lifeworlds. In contrast to the unrestrained creative play of tribes, these fantasy worlds are defined by elaborate performances, rituals and traditions, and the loosely scripted use of objects (Belk and Costa 1998; Seregina 2018). Active involvement and absorption into these fantasy worlds therefore demands extensive learning and skill acquisition (Murphy, Patterson, and O'Malley 2019) and, as a result, provides consumers with intrinsic rewards, social bonding, and peer recognition (Seregina and Weijo 2016). Outside of these immediate pleasures, these fantasy worlds provide consumers with therapeutic respite (Higgins and Hamilton 2018) that enable them to re-enter ordinary life refreshed and revitalized.

Fragility and fitness. A third form of hedonistic distraction is fragility and fitness. This category of experience is characterized by consumers reawakening the body and its associated carnal pleasures and pains through active engagement with nature. In their consideration of the complex embodied learning that underpins extreme sports, Brymer and Gray (2010) stress how surfers, mountaineers, and free-base jumpers are motivated by the desire to break with the boredom of everyday life, which leads them to high-risk activities that foreground the fragility of human life and the overwhelming power of nature (Arnould and Price 1993; Canniford 2012; Canniford and Shankar 2013). Such encounters conjure the 'sublime', which for Kant (1960) refers to the experience of being overpowered yet also elevated. Consider the following from a white-water kayaker recalling a trip in Russia (Brymer and Gray 2010, 367):

> You cannot conquer a river. How can you defeat something that is never the same twice, that is unaware of your presence? To the river, we are so

much flotsam, and if we forget that the results can be decidedly final. It is often difficult to remember the force of the river in places like this; the water can smash a swimmer to pieces on the rocks and leave them broken like a doll or a piece of rubbish bobbing in the backwaters of an eddy.

There was enough force in [the name of a particular rapid] to rip us from our frail craft and pound us like so much drift wood. And the river wouldn't even know we were dead. There can be no competition, no way we can fight against the huge forces we travel in.

Even though such encounters leave consumers stupefied – in awe of the power and force of nature – they nevertheless provide transformative experiences through which they realize something profound about human's relationship to nature. Such experiences bestow a "new perspective on life" (Arnould and Price 1993, 38) and renewed strength with which to attack everyday life. Although interactions with these natural environments appear to provide consumers with a distinctly unique form of distraction, the nature that consumers encounter is specific: it is romantic, anchored to sets of extremes – high and low culture, over-whelmed yet enlightened, the very small, or the overwhelmingly large (Tuan 2013). The natural environments that consumers use to reinvigorate themselves resist human habitation, such as oceans, mountains, and rainforests (Arnould, Price, and Tierney 1998; Tumbat and Belk 2013). The fragility of the body and human civilization that become obvious in these settings remind consumers of the overwhelming potential of nature and our inability to control it – a subtext that motivates mountaineers, big-wave surfers, and base jumpers.

Similar to how those involved in high-risk sports and leisure activities treat the natural world as 'playground' on which to test themselves, consumers seek out more controlled battlegrounds to exert their physical prowess. The most commercially successful of these controlled environments is Tough Mudder, a painful, gruelling, military-style obstacle course that people pay money and place considerable time training to tackle. Scott et al. (2017) explain its popular-ity as stemming from white-collar workers' desire to experience temporary pain and suffering in response to the "corporeal absence that characterizes urban life" (Scott et al. 2017, 17). These conclusions help explain why intense and painful corporeal experiences resonate with the managerial and professional classes of advanced capitalist societies, for it is through extreme and at times painful phys-ical pursuits (Scott, Husemann, and Hill 2019) that 'blot out' (Baumeister 1988, 138) anxieties related to the disembodied nature of work in advanced capitalist societies and service-based economies.

Festival. If facilitating forms of consumer play is at the heart of contemporary business success (O'Sullivan and Shankar 2019; Thrift 2008), then festival is cen-tral to the maintenance of community, nationhood, and the political and social status quo. Festival is a form of "serious play" (Abrahams 1982, 163) character-ized by excessive performances that at time flirt with carnal desire, debauchery, and taboo. Though these performances may be 'authentically staged' (Flinn and

Frew 2014), they may also occur in less controlled and commercial settings. But despite the obvious countercultural associations, festivals are rarely sites of emancipatory or radical change. Events such as *Burning Man* (Kozinets 2002) demonstrate how a festival's radical potential can not only be blunted but also be used as a rejuvenating source that sharpens the leading edge of libertarian, Californian cyber-capitalism (Barbrook and Cameron 1996). Accordingly, festivals provide consumers with the opportunity for temporary release and to experience critical "respite from the mundane world of hard labor, boredom and thrift. ... The joyful energizing that festival affords is carried back into everyday life as an aid to sustenance and hope" (Bradford and Sherry 2015, 132).

Not all festivals are music festivals, and the vast majority of them differ from Burning Man's "toxic brew of psychotropic drugs and hardcore libertarianism" (Orr 2015). As Stone (2008, 220) lists them, there is

> the regional festival, the religious music festival, the urban festival, the holiday destination festival, the premium festival product, the secret festival, the teenagers' festival, the deliberately constrained festival, the boutique festival, the womens' festival, the green festival, the family festival, the dual-location festival, the economy festival, the political festival, the no-camping festival, and the virtual festival.

It is music festivals that prove most popular, resurging across North America and Western Europe. It is difficult to overlook how music festivals provide people with a carved-out time and space to 'lose it' (Goulding et al. 2009) through a cocktail of drugs, drink, and music, which Canniford (2011, 68) describes succinctly through his formula of "rural fields + DJ + sound system + ecstasy + partypeople[n]". But the pleasures derived from music festivals stem from the way in which music is mobilized as a key resource through which individual and collective transcendence is achieved (DeNora 1999; Nuttall 2009; Roy and Dowd 2010). Indeed, Patterson and Larsen (2019, 113) explain the transformative potential of music when they write that "sounds change us... sound reminds us of the elasticity of the self, making evident the continuity and discontinuity of our subjectivity ... and clarifying the connectedness between inside and outside, self and other".

Music festivals also provide consumers with highly valued cultural resources to rework in an age of social media, where lifestyle is networked, digitized, and a resource to solidify current or access future employment opportunities (Flinn and Frew 2014). No longer are music festivals for countercultural outsiders, hippy idealists, or teenagers looking to rebel (Hebdige 1979; Taylor and Cohen 1976). Instead, they are places where those with plenty go to interact with the 'occult' or the 'mystical' while also working, uploading photos of their experiences to social media where these magical mystical moments accrue cultural capital as they circulate to a captive audience of friends and colleagues (Flinn and Frew 2014). Arguably, modern music festivals have forged a unique position in the experience economy (Pine and Gilmore 2011) by striking the right balance between exerting countercultural cool, on the one hand, while simultaneously reflecting contemporary consumerism, on the other hand.

To summarize, marketing and consumer research has sketched out the variety of hedonistic, involved avenues of distraction and temporary escape consumers seek out. Whether it refers to cosplayers or libertarian 'tech-bros' fuelled up to their eyeballs on ketamine in a desert in Nevada, each of these categories has one thing in common: a high degree of consumer absorption and involvement. They have at their heart what Csikszentmihalyi (1990) sketches out as a 'flow' experiences, a phenomenological state in which people are involved and absorbed into a particular activity that directs their attention away from the travails of everyday life. Not only this, they demand considerable time and effort on part of the consumer, and for some degree of informed socialization into the particular consumer activity. For instance, to climb a mountain requires the acquisition of new bodily skills, let alone equipment and tools (Murphy et al. 2019; Tumbat and Belk 2013). Such activities therefore provide consumers with an immersive temporary refuge from whatever state of drudgery and dreariness that currently plagues their ordinary existence.

We now suggest, however, that 24/7 'on-demand' digitized globalized capitalism has found new ways to distract by providing an endless stream of digital stimuli to prevent us from ever having time to truly idle while simultaneously placing us in a state of constant low-level boredom. In doing so, we engage with intimations of boredom associated with the digitization and speeding up of globalized capitalism. To begin with, we introduce boredom as an affective state of disengaged absorption (Anderson 2004).

Bored to distraction

Boredom is an affective state of disengaged absorption (Anderson 2004). Boredom is dual in structure: it is a sensation of disengagement combined with the feeling of absorption. Boredom disengages. A bored person is incapable of engaging fully with the situation at hand or the world around them, deriving nothing from the variety of sensory stimuli they are currently encountering. A bored person can be easily identified. Their elbows rest on tables, supporting their chin and heavy head. Their necks droop. They often yawn.

Boredom is an "experience without qualities" (Goodstein 2005, 1), a disengaged state that drains the life, desire, and libidinal forces out of you, rendering the world inert, as if it lacks any spark or potentiality. It isn't therefore an internal condition, but one that colours the world. As Toohey (2011, 33) writes, "it's a condition that entails a powerful and unrelieved sense of emptiness, isolation and revilement in which the individual feels a persistent lack of interest in, and difficulty with concentrating on, his current circumstances". When bored, time drags on (Woermann and Rokka 2015), a minute feels like an hour, an hour feels like a day (Toohey 2011).

Boredom is also absorbing. As cultural theorist Mark Fisher (2018, 550) writes, boredom is "a state of high absorption, which is why it is such an oppressive feeling". Boredom lingers; it is all-absorbing and all-consuming. Boredom can be chronic, existential, or profound. For Heidegger (1995), boredom is the 'fundamental mood' by virtue of how people cannot see a future outside of it or develop methods to overcome it. Yet being bored is, for Walter Benjamin, part and parcel of modern culture and is the source for positive and creative engagement with the world, a threshold that must be crossed for life to becoming meaningful and for new creations to be forged. As Benjamin (1968, 91) describes, "If sleep is the apogee of physical relaxation, boredom is the apogee of mental relaxation. Boredom is the dream bird that hatches the egg of experience". In other words, profound boredom is a moment in which creative potential must be pooled and sourced, even if it is difficult to see how boredom, when in that moment, can be overcome.

The source of boredom is modernity. Artistic, literary, and cultural artefacts and histories of the nineteenth century are packed with depictions of environments, situations, and people that appear disengaged, dull, without colour or life (Haladyn and Gardiner 2017). Boredom is a persistent symptom of the "visual culture, mass society, mass production and consumerism" (Petro 2000, 30) that started its development in the late nineteenth century. Gardiner (2012, 41) traces boredom to the entanglement of two social and cultural transformations to occur in this period:

> the 'twin revolutions' of industrialization and the French Republic. The first is a process of cultural modernization that devalues the past, stressing instead perpetual change, innovation and transformation vis-a-vis both self and world. The second is an increasingly standardized form of social existence, which is under continuous assault from the acceleration and redeployment of temporality that is the crux of modernization.

If boredom is the necessary corollary of industrialized capitalism, then how has this 'experience without qualities' been ignored by marketing and consumer researchers? Boredom can be boring to write about, despite the fact that it seems to be a phenomenological state we can all too readily fall into. Boredom is an affective state that does not neatly fit into any of the standardly recognized categories of consumer experience, and that it bears greater resemblance to other types of curious, ephemeral, difficult-to-speak of 'non-representational' things (Hill, Canniford, and Mol 2014) that seem to arise in particular situations and are non-localizable and whose source is unclear and indeterminate, such as the atmosphere of a busy coffee shop in which a space is filled "with a certain of feeling like a haze" (Biehl-Missal and Saren 2012; Böhme 1993, 114; Hill 2016; Kotler 1973). Indeed, boredom is neither an internal subjective state nor an immutable property of an object. Instead, boredom radiates from the environment as much as the people who are in a state of boredom and, consequently, defies the mechanistic worldviews of mainstream marketing and consumer research (Arnould and Thompson 2005) while also flying under the radar in first-person, interview-based research methods that define qualitative marketing and consumer research (Hill et al. 2014).

Boredom as the defining affective state of contemporary capitalism

Despite consumer capitalism promising to eliminate boredom, it is yet to be vanquished. Even with the smartphone, a device that promises unlimited convenience and entertainment in most consumers' fingertips, cultural theorists explain "the feeling most characteristic of our current moment is a mixture of boredom and compulsion" (Fisher 2018, 550). And even with the proliferation of on-demand subscription-based services – Netflix, Amazon Prime, and so on – that form an integral part of today's media landscape (Bardhi and Eckhardt 2017; Russell and Levy 2012), the rediscovery and release of old and new television programmes, documentaries, and film fail to deliver anything new or different. And yet these services remain more popular than ever.

One survey suggests that UK adults spend, on average, 12 hours a week glued to a screen, binging on boxsets (Perraudin 2018). Indeed, there is always another platform to subscribe to, a new series that extends the storyline, a different boxset to tune into, and always another episode to watch before bed. Subscription television provider Sky plays with intimations of boredom and on-demand 24/7 services in their advertisements for Sky boxsets. Across a series of advertisements, Idris Elba champions Sky's endless choice. In one, he walks along a corridor of white shelves, each one filled with DVD cases with people admonishing their friends for missing the latest episode, or not even being familiar with one of the latest titles. In 2014 this innovation brought seemingly endless choice for the Sky subscriber with the announcement on 14 February (LBBOnline 2014) that

> From today, millions of Sky customers will be able to access even more TV box sets on demand, including full series of 24, Modern Family, Girls and Bones. This builds on the rapid expansion of the service throughout 2013, during which time the number of hours of TV box sets available on Sky has more than doubled. TV fans are now able to enjoy more TV box sets of the latest shows on demand through Sky than they can through any other UK pay TV or online subscription service.
>
> More than 4 million connected Sky homes already enjoy access to a great range of top TV box sets to watch whenever they want, including An Idiot Abroad, Banshee, Castle, Criminal Minds, The Following, Luther, Mad Dogs, Misfits, Moone Boy, Peep Show, Stella, A Touch of Cloth, A Young Doctor's Notebook, and The Wire.

We focus on Elba's Sky television adverts to designate a broader shift in how the contemporary version of capitalism is typified by content and entertainment that provides a never-ending stream of stimuli that prevent consumers from ever being 'switched off', not to declare that we are living in an age of 'digital plenitude' (Bolter 2019) or golden age of media entertainment. Instead, we take Mark Fisher's analysis (2018, 550) seriously when he writes that "in the intensive, 24/7 environment of capitalist cyberspace, the brain is no longer allowed any time to idle, instead, it is inundated with a seamless flow of low-level stimulus". Boredom is the 'structure of feeling' (Williams 1977) that defines our contemporary period.

The multiplication of screens, on-demand television services, and social media has created changes in the affective quality of contemporary capitalism. It cannot be overstated how much the smartphone is responsible for this transformation (Greenfield 2017). For many, the device is the last thing put down before sleep and the first thing picked up in the morning. They are used to plug downtime of 30 seconds to two hours. They plug us into work and into entertainment services, with content providers developing elaborate and sophisticated apps to enable consumers to access entertainment while they are in bed, on the toilet, or on public transport.

It is impossible for consumers to fall into what Heidegger (1995) termed 'profound boredom', a sense of 'doing nothing' that sparks people to use their unsettled experience of the world around them for ethical self-reflection (Benjamin 1968; Hand 2017). Instead, there is always a social media channel to flick through, a photo to upload, a comment to make, a quiz to do, a Facebook argument to enter, a kitten to smile to, and a new television series to pay little attention to while doing all of the above. In short, there is an abundance of stimuli that while not provoking an engaged and absorbed response instead temporarily occupies our minds and bodies that place consumers in a state of boredom.

To end this chapter, we explore the social forces that explain why this boredom is the dominant affective state of our era and the contemporary form of distraction. To do this, we sketch the contours of digitized 24/7 'on-demand' globalized capitalism by outlining two key vectors in the intensification of boredom, acceleration, and connectivity.

Acceleration

Within recent cultural and social theory, relationships between the organization and experience of time and globalized capitalism have received considerable attention. Terms such as 'speed' and 'acceleration' have been used to describe the distinctive temporality associated with globalized capitalism (Husemann and Eckhardt 2019; Rosa and Scheurman 2009; Rosa and Trejo-Mathys 2013; Virilio 1986). Underpinning these terms is the idea that time is 'compressed' and 'desequenced' (Castells 2009) as a result of the 'economic logic of capitalism'

(Rosa 2005, 448). This logic, as Marx (1848) explains, prioritizes change over conservatism and innovation over stasis:

> The bourgeoisie cannot exist without constantly revolutionizing the instruments of production, and thereby the relations of production, and with them the relations of society as a whole. Conservation of the old modes of production in unaltered form, was, on the contrary, the first condition of existence for all earlier industrial classes. Constant revolutionizing of production, uninterrupted disturbance of all social conditions, everlasting uncertainty and movement distinguish the bourgeois epoch from all earlier ones. All fixed, fast-frozen relations, with their train of ancient and venerable prejudices and opinions, are swept away, all new-formed ones become antiquated before they can ossify. All that is solid melts into air, all that is holy is profaned.

The systemic tendency of capitalism to accelerate corresponds to the intensification of time that people feel, experience, and discuss. For it appears that acceleration is part and parcel of commercially led developments that above all else seek to increase the speed and flow of resources central to capitalism: technological innovations that make us more productive at work and technological developments that promise to get products to us quicker than ever before (Rosa 2005; Rosa and Scheurman 2009). Indeed, Amazon's Prime Air advertisements featuring *Top Gear* presenter Jeremy Clarkson declare that you can "have them delivered in thirty minutes or less, and in a location not so far away, a miracle of technology is dispatched, it's an Amazon drone". These adverts do little to dispel the idea that Amazon finds little wrong with clogging streets with delivery vehicles and colonizing the air (and sea, if we are to take their patent to use lakes and reservoirs as dispatching centres at face value (see Walter 2017)).

Acceleration helps explain the prevalence of boredom in two ways. First, acceleration eliminates 'downtime'. Capitalism is not just spatially extensive, spreading globally, but temporally intensive, increasing the speed with which tasks need to be completed, filling this temporal gap with more tasks (Beer 2019). And the passing time between each task has been decreased, if not eliminated entirely. As a result, the sense, pleasure, and opportunity of 'doing nothing' have been simply eradicated. Without this, the remaining short amount of time people have at hand is filled with activities that take little time. As such, people spend their time scrolling and thumbing through digital social network updates, linking, tagging, and commenting, ultimately in order to maintain a 'digital' version of the self for work and social networks (Arvidsson and Caliandro 2016; Bardhi and Eckhardt 2017; Belk 2013).

Second, acceleration causes leisure and work to blend into one another. As such, work emails are received, read, and responded to during 'leisure' time. But this does not mean it isn't possible to be bored. Instead, it means it isn't possible to ever engage and be absorbed into a single piece of media for a considerable amount of time. Following the release of Martin Scorsese's film, *The Irishman*, on

Netflix in November 2019, social media users boasted about how many sittings it took for them to finish a film 3 hours and 30 minutes in length. While some put this length down to Scorsese's eye for meticulous detail, others explained that 210 minutes is simply too long to not be interacting with other forms of media, and that it is simply too difficult to 'un-connect' yourself from digital devices for that amount of time.

Connectivity

Alongside acceleration then is the process of connectivity that makes it impossible for people to escape digital media and technologically mediated distraction. Consumers are always 'plugged into' a digital network that remains largely invisible, placed at the centre of a data gaze that operates continually, collecting facts about ourselves without our noticing and turning these insights into managerially relevant actions (Beer 2019).

Over the past 25 years, digital devices, sensors, and complex infrastructures have penetrated work life as much as they have colonized home life (Hoffman and Novak 2018). Smart cities always monitor, smart speakers always listen, and smartphones are always receiving. The proliferation of devices that constantly vie for our attention, focus, and touch continues to increase, placing us into positions of 24/7 connectivity with technological systems. As Judy Wajcman (2015, 1) says, "the technologically tethered, iPhone-addicted figure is an image we can easily conjure. Most of us complain there aren't enough hours in the day and that there are too many e-mails in our thumb-accessible inboxes". The time we have to direct our attention to a single task or thing continues to decline. Interruptions emerge from different devices and screens and from different people. The net result is an endless stream of disruptions to break our "flow of consciousness that disrupt whatever activity we happen to be pursuing" (Rosa and Scheurman 2009, 2).

As intimated before in this chapter, smartphones are key to understanding how people become tethered to 24/7 digital capitalism, for they plug us into a digitized system of constant stimulation and distraction typified by an array of low-impact stimuli (Greenfield 2017; Turkle 2015). For they constitute a device through which individuals become networked, connected such that work bleeds into leisure time, even into our sleep (Crary 2013). Smartphones allow the news to come to us, wherever we may be and whatever time it is. It allows us to shop whenever we wish. It allows us to purchase whichever cryptocurrency is currently being peddled. The smartphone therefore enables the world to be "reimagined as a non-stop work site or an always open shopping mall of infinite choices, tasks, selections and digressions" (Crary 2013, 17).

Smartphone manufacturers stress this unlimited potential in their advertisements, reifying the benefits that accrue from being constantly plugged into 24/7 digital capitalism. *Samsung* promoted its Galaxy S10 handset with the benefit of 'Next Generation Connectivity', which means that the

> S10 is built for tomorrow. Wi-Fi 6 makes it the first mobile to connect you quicker and more securely to the content you love. And because we've pioneered next generation connectivity, for a generation that can't wait, S10 is also the first to offer super-fast 5G, ensuring you're always connected, wherever, whenever.

Yet it is difficult to 'unplug', and there are clear disincentives that prevent people from binning this mobile technology. As Greenfield (2017, 24) explains, "those who enjoy access to networked services are more capable than those without". The smartphone is our map, our ID card, our debit card, our radio, our newspaper, our radio, our weatherman, and our handheld television. Despite the growth in a genre of products and services that promise a 'digital detox' (Husemann and Eckhardt 2019), these are nevertheless temporary escapes. Yet by remaining plugged into these digital networks, the cost is clear. For it means that the time we have at our disposal to focus on any single thing continues to diminish. It means we are incessantly interrupted by a torrent of messages, updates, news, and photographs, where even the tiny 'ding' of a notification alert can interfere with whatever it is that we are currently pursuing. And while this connection allows us to have everything to choose from, there is paradoxically nothing of substance for us to engage in, placing us in a state of low-level boredom.

Bibliography

Abrahams, Roger (1982), "The Language of Festivals: Celebrating the Economy," in *Celebration Studies in Festivity and Ritual*, ed. Victor Turner, Washington, DC: Smithsonian Institution Press, 161–89.

Anderson, Ben (2004), "Time-Stilled Space-Slowed: How Boredom Matters," *Geoforum*, 35(6), 739–54.

Arnould, Eric J. and Linda L. Price (1993), "River Magic: Extraordinary Experience and the Extended Service Encounter," *Journal of Consumer Research*, 20(1), 24–45.

Arnould, Eric J., Linda L. Price, and Patrick Tierney (1998), "Communicative Staging of the Wilderness Servicescape," *The Service Industries Journal*, 18(3), 90–115.

Arnould, Eric J. and Craig J. Thompson (2005), "Consumer Culture Theory (CCT): Twenty Years of Research," *Journal of Consumer Research*, 31(4), 868–82.

Arvidsson, Adam and Alessandro Caliandro (2016), "Brand Public," *Journal of Consumer Research*, 42(5), 727–48.

Barbrook, Richard and Andy Cameron (1996), "The Californian Ideology," *Science as Culture*, 6(1), 44–72.

Bardhi, Fleura and Giana M. Eckhardt (2017), "Liquid Consumption," eds. Eileen Fischer and Deborah J MacInnis, *Journal of Consumer Research*, 44(3), 582–97.

Baumeister, Roy F. (1988), "Masochism as Escape from Self," *The Journal of Sex Research*, 25(1), 28–59.

Beer, David (2019), *The Data Gaze: Capitalism, Power and Perception*, London: SAGE.

Belk, Russell W. (2013), "Extended Self in a Digital World: Table 1," *Journal of Consumer Research*, 40(3), 477–500.

Belk, Russell W. and Janeen Arnold Costa (1998), "The Mountain Man Myth: A Contemporary Consuming Fantasy," *Journal of Consumer Research*, 25(3), 218–40.

Benjamin, Walter (1968), "The Storyteller," in *Illuminations: Essays and Reflections*, Trans. Harry Zohn, New York: Schocken Books, 83–109.

Biehl-Missal, Brigitte and Michael Saren (2012), "Atmospheres of Seduction: A Critique of Aesthetic Marketing Practices," *Journal of Macromarketing*, 32(2), 168–80.

Böhme, Gernot (1993), "Atmosphere as the Fundamental Concept of a New Aesthetics," *Thesis Eleven*, 36, 113–26.

Bolter, J. David (2019), *The Digital Plenitude: The Decline of Elite Culture and the Rise of Digital Media*, Cambridge, MA: The MIT Press.

Bradford, Tonya Williams and John F. Sherry (2015), "Domesticating Public Space through Ritual: Tailgating as Vestaval," *Journal of Consumer Research*, 42(1), 130–51.

Brymer, Eric and Tonia Gray (2010), "Developing an Intimate 'Relationship' with Nature through Extreme Sports Participation," *Leisure/Loisir*, 34(4), 361–74.

Caillois, Roger (1950), *L'homme et Le Sacré*, Paris: Gallimard.

Canniford, Robin (2011), "How to Manage Consumer Tribes," *Journal of Strategic Marketing*, 19(5), 453–68.

——— (2012), "Poetic Witness: Marketplace Research through Poetic Transcription and Poetic Translation," *Marketing Theory*, 12(4), 391–409.

Canniford, Robin and Avi Shankar (2013), "Purifying Practices: How Consumers Assemble Romantic Experiences of Nature," *Journal of Consumer Research*, 39(5), 1051–69.

Castells, Manuel (2009), *The Rise of the Network Society*, 1, Second Edition, Oxford: Blackwell.

Cova, Bernard and Daniele Dalli (2009), "Working Consumers: The next Step in Marketing Theory?," *Marketing Theory*, 9(3), 315–39.

Cova, Bernard, Robert V. Kozinets, and Avi Shankar, eds. (2007), *Tribes, Inc.*, Oxford: Elsevier.

Crary, Jonathan (2013), *24/7: Late Capitalism and the Ends of Sleep*, London: Verso.

Csikszentmihalyi, Mihaly (1990), *Flow: The Psychology of Optimal Experience*, New York: Harper and Row.

DeNora, Tia (1999), "Music as a Technology of the Self," *Poetics*, 27(1), 31–56.

Fisher, Mark (2018), *K-Punk: The Collection and Unpublished Writings of Mark Fisher (2004–2016)*, edited by Darren Ambrose, London: Repeater Books.

Flinn, Jenny and Matt Frew (2014), "Glastonbury: Managing the Mystification of Festivity," *Leisure Studies*, 33(4), 418–33.

Gardiner, M. E. (2012), "Henri Lefebvre and the 'Sociology of Boredom,' " *Theory, Culture and Society*, 29(2), 57–62.

Goodstein, Elisabeth S. (2005), *Experience without Qualities: Boredom and Modernity*, Stanford University Press.

Greenfield, Adam (2017), *Radical Technologies: The Design of Everyday Life*, London: Verso.

Haladyn, Julian Jason and Michael E. Gardiner (2017), "Monotonous Splendour: An Introduction to Boredom Studies," in *Boredom Studies Reader: Frameworks and Perspectives*, eds. Michael E. Gardiner and Julian Jason Haladyn, Abingdon, Oxon: Routledge, 1–16.

Hand, Martin (2017), "Boredom. Technology, Acceleration and Connected Presence in Social Media Age," in *Boredom Studies Reader: Frameworks and Perspecptives*, eds. Michael E. Gardiner and Julian Jason Haladyn, London: Routledge, 127–41.

Hargadon, Andrew (2003), *How Breakthrough Happens*, Boston, MA: Harvard Business Review Press.

Hebdige, Dick (1979), *Subculture: The Meaning of Style*, London: Routledge.

Heidegger, Martin (1995), *The Fundametal Concepts of Metaphysics: World, Finitude, Solitude*, Bloomington, IN: Indiana University Press.

Held, David (1990), *Introduction to Critical Theory: Horkheimer to Habermas*, Cambridge: Polity Press.

Higgins, Leighanne and Kathy Hamilton (2018), "Therapeutic Servicescapes and Market-Mediated Performances of Emotional Suffering," eds. Eileen Fischer and Craig Thompson, *Journal of Consumer Research*, https://academic.oup.com/jcr/advance-article/doi/10.1093/jcr/ucy046/4995181.

Hill, Tim (2016), "Mood-Management in the English Premier League," in *Assembling Consumption: Researching Actors, Networks and Markets*, eds. Robin Canniford and Domen Bajde, London: Routledge, 155–71.

Hill, Tim, Robin Canniford, and Joeri Mol (2014), "Non-Representational Marketing Theory," *Marketing Theory*, 14(4), 377–94.

Hoffman, Donna L. and Thomas P. Novak (2018), "Consumer and Object Experience in the Internet of Things: An Assemblage Theory Approach," *Journal of Consumer Research*, 44(6), 1178–204.

Holbrook, Morris B. and Elizabeth C. Hirschman (1982), "The Experiential Aspects of Consumption: Consumer Fantasies, Feelings, and Fun," *Journal of Consumer Research*, 9(2), 132–40.

Horkheimer, Max and Theodor W. Adorno (1996), *Dialectic of Enlightenment*, New York: Continuum.

Husemann, Katharina C. and Giana M. Eckhardt (2019), "Consumer Deceleration," *Journal of Consumer Research*, 45(6), 1142–63.

Kant, Immanuel (1960), *Observations on the Feeling of the Beautiful and Sublime*, Berkeley, CA: University of California Press.

Kotler, Phillip (1973), "Atmospherics as Marketing Tool," *Journal of Retailing*, 49(4), 48–84.

Kozinets, Robert V. (2001), "Utopian Enterprise: Articulating the Meanings of Star Trek's Culture of Consumption," *Journal of Consumer Research*, 28(1), 67–88.

———— (2002), "Can Consumers Escape the Market? Emancipatory Illuminations from Burning Man," *Journal of Consumer Research*, 29(1), 20–38.

Lasch, Christopher (1979), *The Culture of Narcissism: American Life in an Age of Diminishing Expectations*, New York: W. W. Norton & Company.

LBBOnline (2014), "Idris Elba Stars for Sky Box Sets | LBBOnline," https://lbbonline.com/news/idris-elba-stars-for-sky-box-sets/.

Lears, T.J. Jackson (1983), "From Salvation to Self-Realization: Advertising and the Therapeautic Roots of the Consumer Culture, 1880–1930," in *The Culture of Consumption: Critical Essays in American History, 1880–1980*, eds. Richard W. Fox and T.J. Jackson Lears, New York: Partheon Books, 3–38.

Mamali, Elizabeth, Peter Nuttall, and Avi Shankar (2018), "Formalizing Consumer Tribes: Towards a Theorization of Consumer-Constructed Organizations," *Marketing Theory*, 18(4), 521–42.

Martin, Richard (1995), "Gay Blades: Homoerotic Content in J. C. Leyendecker's Gillette Advertising Images," *Journal of American Culture*, 18(2), 75–82.

Marx, Karl and Friedrich Engels (1848), *The Communist Manifesto*, London: Penguin.

Molesworth, Mike and Denigri-Knott Janice (2008), "The Playfulness of EBay and the Implications for Business as a Game-Maker," *Journal of Macromarketing*, 28(4), 369–80.

Muñiz, Albert M. and Thomas C. O'Guinn (2001), "Brand Community," *Journal of Consumer Research*, 27(4), 412–32.

Muñiz, Albert M. and Hope Jensen Schau (2005), "Reliogisity in the Abandoned Apple Newton Brand Community," *Journal of Consumer Research*, 31(4), 737–47.

Murphy, Stephen, Maurice Patterson, and Lisa O'Malley (2019), "Learning How: Body Techniques, Skill Acquisition and the Consumption of Experience," *Marketing Theory*, 19(4), 425–45.

Nuttall, Pete (2009), "Insiders, Regulars and Tourists: Exploring Selves and Music Consumption in Adolescence," *Journal of Consumer Behaviour*, 8(4), 211–24.

Orazi, Davide C. and Angela Gracia B. Cruz (2019), "LARPnography: An Embodied Embedded Cognition Method to Probe the Future," *European Journal of Marketing*, 53(8), 1637–64.

Orr, Niela (2015), "Town without Purpose," *The Baffler*, https://thebaffler.com/latest/bud-light.

O'Sullivan, Stephen R. and Avi Shankar (2019), "Rethinking Marketplace Culture: Play and the Context of Context," *Marketing Theory*, 19(4), 509–31.

Patterson, Maurice and Gretchen Larsen (2019), "Listening to Consumption: Towards a Sonic Turn in Consumer Research," *Marketing Theory*, 19(2), 105–27.

Peñaloza, Lisa (2001), "Consuming the American West: Animating Cultural Meaning and Memory at a Stock Show and Rodeo," *Journal of Consumer Research*, 28(3), 369–98.

Perraudin, Frances (2018), "Average Briton Spends 26 Days a Year Watching On-Demand TV," *The Guardian*, September 23, https://www.theguardian.com/society/2018/sep/23/average-briton-spends-26-days-a-year-watching-on-demand-tv-survey.

Petro, P.S. (2000), "Boredom," *Public: An Interdisicplinary Journal of Art, Culture, and Ideas*, 19(1), 30–31.

Pine, B. Joseph and James H. Gilmore (2011), *The Experience Economy*, Boston, MA: Harvard Business Press.

Roffe, Jon (2020), *The Works of Gilles Deleuze I: 1953–1969*, Melbourne: re.press.

Rosa, Harmut (2005), "The Speed of Global Flows and the Pace of Democratic Politics," *New Political Science*, 27(4), 445–59.

Rosa, Hartmut and William E. Scheurman, eds. (2009), *High-Speed Society: Social Acceleration, Power and Modernity*, University Park, PA: Penn State University Press.

Rosa, Hartmut and Jonathan Trejo-Mathys (2013), *Social Acceleration: A New Theory of Modernity*, New York: Columbia University Press.

Roy, William G. and Timothy J. Dowd (2010), "What Is Sociological about Music?," *Annual Review of Sociology*, 36(1), 183–203.

Russell, Cristel Antonia and Sidney J. Levy (2012), "The Temporal and Focal Dynamics of Volitional Reconsumption: A Phenomenological Investigation of Repeated Hedonic Experiences," *Journal of Consumer Research*, 39(2), 341–59.

Scott, Rebecca, Julien Cayla, and Bernard Cova (2017), "Selling Pain to the Saturated Self," eds. Eileen Fischer and Robert Kozinets, *Journal of Consumer Research*, 44(1), 22–43.

Scott, Rebecca, Katharina C. Husemann, and Tim Hill (2019), "Identity Verification through Pain in Extraordinary Consumer Experiences," in *Handbook of Research on Identity Theory in Marketing*, eds. Americus Reed II and Mark Forehand, London: Edward Elgar Publishing, 255–69.

Seregina, Usva (2018), *Performing Fantasy and Reality in Contemporary Culture*, London: Routledge.

Seregina, Usva and Henri A. Weijo (2016), "Play at Any Cost: How Cosplayers Produce and Sustain Their Ludic Communal Consumption Experiences," *Journal of Consumer Research*, 44(1), 139–59.

Stone, Chris (2008), The British pop music festival phenomenon. *International Perspectives of Festivals and Events*, 205–24.

Taylor, Laurie and Stanley Cohen (1976), *Escape Attempts: The Theory and Practice of Resistance to Everyday Life*, London: Allen Lane.

Thrift, Nigel (2008), *Non-Representational Theory: Space, Politics, Affect*, Routledge: Abingdon.

Toohey, Peter (2011), *Boredom: A Lively History*, London: Yale University Press.

Tuan, Yi-Fu (2013), *Romantic Geography: In Search of the Sublime Landscape*, Madison, WI: The University of Wisconsin Press.

Tumbat, Gülnur and Russell W. Belk (2013), "Co-construction and Performancescapes: Co-construction and Performancescapes," *Journal of Consumer Behaviour*, 12(1), 49–59.

Turkle, Shelly (2015), *Reclaiming Conversation*, New York: Penguin.

Virilio, Paul (1986), *Speed and Politics: An Essay on Dromology*, New York: Semiotext(e).

Wajcman, Judy (2015), *Pressed for Time: The Acceleration of Life in Digital Capitalism*, Chicago, IL: The University of Chicago Press.

Walter, Alexander (2017), "Amazon's Patent for 'Aquatic Storage Facilities' Could Turn Lakes into Underwater Warehouses," *Archinect*, https://archinect.com/news/article/150017459/amazon-s-patent-for-aquatic-storage-facilities-could-turn-lakes-into-underwater-warehouses.

Weijo, Henri A., Diane M. Martin, and Eric J. Arnould (2018), "Consumer Movements and Collective Creativity: The Case of Restaurant Day," eds. Eileen Fischer and Guliz Ger, *Journal of Consumer Research*, 45(2), 251–74.

Williams, Raymond (1977), *Marxism and Literature*, Oxford: Oxford University Press.

——— (1980), "Advertising: The Magic System," in *Problems in Materialism and Culture*, London: Verso, 170–95.

Williamson, J. (1978), *Decoding Advertisements: Ideology and Meaning in Advertising*, London: Marion Boyers.

Woermann, Niklas and Joonas Rokka (2015), "Timeflow: How Consumption Practices Shape Consumers' Temporal Experiences," *Journal of Consumer Research*, 41(6), 1486–508.

Žižek, Slavoj (1997), *The Plague of Fantasies*, London: Verso.

8

AFTERWORD

How does this end?

Globalized capitalism is currently disintegrating, but there is nothing on the horizon to immediately replace it. We are in an *interregnum* (Gramsci 1971), a period defined by radical uncertainty in which dissent and radical politics flourish. Capitalism has always found ways to repair itself at previous times of crisis (Streeck 2017; Wallerstein et al. 2013). To understand some of the ways in which globalized capitalism has sought to fight back against its demise, this book has, in the style of picaresque novella *Lazarillo de Tormes*, turned the spotlight on five logics that lurk behind and animate marketing communications since the global financial crisis. In doing so, this book has sought to re-politicize the study of marketing communications in order to not only diagnose some defining and harmful characteristics of our present moment but also demonstrate some of the ways in which marketing communications keeps globalized capitalism ticking over for the time being. And it is marketing communication's ability to uphold this interregnum is its *dark side*, since it prevents alternative, more equitable, and morally just systems of ordering social life from developing.

Any project influenced by the critical tradition must also go further than diagnosis and critique. It must be concerned with questions and processes of emancipatory social transformation (Murray and Ozanne 1991; Tadajewski and Brownlie 2009; Wright 2010). That is, the gaps, spaces, and opportunities that exist in the social order through which new and alternative future possibilities are made. And although "the pragmatic problems involved in actually connecting with and changing society are indeed great" (Murray and Ozanne 1991, 142), the Leninist question *'what is to be done?'* must be addressed. To do so is to provide answers for key questions that orient this book: how can we get out of globalized capitalism's *interregnum*? Where is the new political common sense going to arrive from? And in what spaces might an alternative future develop?

To this end, this afterword develops a conceptual framework to identify the spaces in which alternative futures can be developed. These form a set of ideas to help understand where transformative change can be potentially located. This doesn't mean we predict what this new political, economic, or social common sense will look like, nor does it mean that we develop a general theory of social reproduction or transformation. Instead, this chapter focusses on the role of two actors in the development of alternative futures: the individual consumer and groups of consumers that form social movements (Gollnhofer, Weijo, and Schouten 2019; Kozinets and Handelman 2004; Varman and Belk 2009; Weijo, Martin, and Arnould 2018). Each, we suggest, carries specific potential towards societal transformation. We do not suggest, however, that each operating by themselves is enough to usher in an alternative politics. Instead, they should be treated as operating more effectively as a configuration in which the interaction between these actors and the state results in a greater level of effectiveness (Wright 2010).

This afterword we hope displays our scepticism towards the tone present across social theory generally and consumer culture theory specifically that is doubtful of whether radical social transformation is desirable or possible. This radical pessimism forecloses consideration of an alternative future outside of globalized capitalism and is a likely consequence of the way in which Baudrillard (1970) and certain interpretations of Foucault (1977, 1980) have had a lasting influence on the heteroglossia that comprises marketing and consumer research (Arnould and Thompson 2005; Thompson, Arnould, and Giesler 2013). "It is hard to imagine a realistic alternative", outside market capitalism writes Arnould (2007, 104), a statement that stresses the conviction that there are few alternative modes of social organization that are desirable or feasible (see also Kozinets 2002; Murray 2002). While there is little doubt that specific worldviews can appear so taken for granted and powerful that it is difficult to imagine how other possible futures can be imagined let alone developed, one of the opportunities that stem from our current interregnum is to try to understand where we may find alternatives to globalized capitalism and how they may become dominant.

Consumers, construers, and the politicization of subjectivity

Of all actors, it is the individual consumer that marketing and consumer research has paid most attention to when trying to understand how radical alternative futures may be created. Whether for reasons of methodological individualism or the discipline's specific historical development (Fitchett, Patsiaouras, and Davies 2014; Thompson et al. 2013), consumer researchers have pronounced the individual consumer as a potential agent of transformation. Of course, individual consumers can change little systematically through what they do or do not purchase or use, for there are a host of institutions that work to actively reproduce the logics of globalized capitalism. This isn't to suggest, however, that there is no purpose or power to a strategy of individual resistance. As we now emphasize, the politicization of consumer subjectivity concerns three interrelated steps: (1) the development of code consciousness, or knowledge of how marketing communications works to conceal, distort, and bestow false properties upon commodities; (2) acts of refusal in which code consciousness is harnessed to reject, break with, and consciously refuse to be complicit in the current system of social order; and (3) the concoction of feasible and desirable blueprints for future forms of social order.

Ozanne and Murray (1995) declare that emancipation and social transformation first must arrive through individual reflexivity, which refers to the ability to revise our understanding of our relationship to nature and social relations. As they explain, consumers "must become more radically critical or reflexively defiant by dropping this natural attitude toward the existing order and, instead, questioning economic, political and social structures" (Ozanne and Murray 1995, 516). Doing so requires a *code* consciousness (Holt 2002) or knowledge that allows consumers to see through the system of cultural meanings that institutions, organizations, and brand encode into commodities (Hall 1997).

This entails learning the tricks of the 'magic system' (Williams 1980). Accordingly, the first step in the politicization of consumer subjectivity is to first become aware of how marketing communications not only distorts and conceals but also marshals a host of cultural and symbolic resources to transform goods and services into objects with magical and life-enhancing properties (Holt 2002; Ozanne and Murray 1995). As Williams (1980, 178) explains, advertising

> associate[s] consumption with human desires to which it has no real reference. You do not only buy an object: you buy social respect, discrimination, health, beauty, success, power to control your environment. The magic obscures the real sources of general satisfaction because their discovery would involve radical change in the whole common way of life.

The power of advertising is that it helps create a symbolically rich world that is teeming with a variety of identities to adopt and personas to live through, but this is a world that is predominantly forged by the hands of marketers (Fırat and Dholakia 2017). We live in an era where minor celebrities and influencers wield considerable clout – with reality television stars endorsing diet drinks that contain cyanide (McLaren 2019); there are plenty of codes for consumers to become sensitive to.

We can also see how becoming code-conscious leads to acts of refusal, "a deliberate move toward one thing, belief, practice, or community and away from another" (McGranahan 2016, 319). By politicizing everyday action, acts of refusal reject the status quo and remove people from participation in harmful acts or their involvement in systems of dominance (Graeber 2013). In *The Gift*, Marcell Mauss (1967) considers acts of refusal as actions through which social relations are cut, generating new forms of social relations and the potential obligations these novel relationships entail. Acts of refusal are not then wholly negative actions that simply look to neutralize the harms of the status quo but are also generative. On this, McGranahan (2016, 322) explains that "the ending of one thing is often the generation of something new". This creative, generative potential of refusal can be witnessed in spontaneous public festivals, where refusing to comply to state regulations results in the formation of new, civic minded community (Weijo et al. 2018). Here, simple acts of refusal and their implicit critique of the status quo provide new and meaningful affiliations between Helsinki residents. Yet becoming code conscious and acts of refusal represent defensive manoeuvres that have individual consumers at their centre. It is therefore important to extend our thinking beyond these reactive acts of resistance and consider offensive strategies that seek to develop blueprints that would provide alternative forms of organizing society (Wright 2019).

Recently, Firat and Dholakia (2017, 515) have suggested that recent technological and cultural developments have ushered in new opportunities for the individual consumer to "focus on 'what is possible' rather than 'what is' ….. the construer subject may be expected to focus on contributing to a culture of presenting the possible". This is a form of consumer subjectivity that seeks to symbolically and materially invent the future outside of the existing paradigm. "The 'chains to lose' – to use a Marxian metaphor", they write, "are in the temporary contemporary imaginary that conditions us into complacency; but these also have the seeds to trigger new imaginaries" (Firat and Dholakia 2017, 518). Harnessing this radical potential would likely involve exploiting the power of 'maker culture' (Anderson 2013): participatory innovation, collaborative design, open-source designs and the knowledge commons, and the democratization of production through three-dimensional printing and additive manufacturing (Greenfield 2017; Srnicek and Williams 2016). Not only this, it would also require the formation of an alternative 'symbolic culture' (Firat and Dholakia 2017, 517) that would allow this alternative to exist and flourish in those that are involved in these future-building experiments, for symbolic culture gives vibrancy, clarity, and weight to these fictional futures (Godelier 2020).

Notwithstanding the transformative potential of individual subjectivity, we add that these imaginaries, whatever their content, have a greater chance of becoming actually existing forms of radical social change when they are shared by a community of people who are invested in its future. Indeed, as Ozanne and Murray (1995, 523) reflect, "only an organized movement of reflexively defiant consumers has the potential to act as an agent [of social transformation]". It is for this reason that marketing and consumer research has taken interest in the activities of politicized groups of consumers who act in manners akin to social movements.

Social movements, interstitial metamorphosis, and real utopias

Marketing and consumer researchers describe how indignant and motivated consumers can target specific organizations (Hill, Canniford, and Millward 2018;

Scaraboto and Fischer 2013; Thompson, Rindfleisch, and Arsel 2006; Varman and Belk 2009). From Coca-Cola to the Premier League, to fashion outlets and global coffee brands, consumers deploy a combination of persuasive and disruptive techniques in order to transform the principles and practices upon which an organization operates (King and Pearce 2010). The persuasive side of these techniques involves the creation and communication of a movement's general message, argument, and aims (Benford and Snow 2000). Movements often target the media, since they comprise the "link between public events and the public sphere" (Oliver and Myers 1999, 38) in ways that place extra pressure on organizations to respond and to create broader support from new audiences (Castells 2015; Koopmans 2004). Disruptive techniques, however, seek to persuade not through words and argument but through by placing limits on an organization's ability to operate desirably, effectively, and efficiently. This includes different kinds of direct action (Kauffman 2017), blocking roads, digital cyberattacks, and strikes.

Other groups of consumers, however, have larger aims, seeking to overturn, transform, and radically change existing economic and social relations. Kozinets and Handelman (2004, 691), for instance, describe how consumers form groups that "attempt to transform various elements of the social order surrounding consumption and marketing". These groups are typically "serious, aloof, … puritanical" (Kozinets and Handelman 2004, 702) and too easily fall into the trap of painting ordinary consumers as brainwashed morons, susceptible to any marketing nonsense. It is therefore little surprise that these groups remain unsuccessful, small, and ostracized.

Yet dismissing these efforts as toothless runs the risk of overlooking the way in which these groups can spawn localized, alternative economies (Campana, Chatzidakis, and Laamanen 2017) and involvement in more radical and experiments that respond to the challenges to peak oil and climate change (Kenis and Mathijs 2014; North and Longhurst 2013). These 'real utopias' (Wright 2010) do not depend upon the state, and notwithstanding their minor differences, eco-villages, de-growth movements, and transition towns share common ground: they seek to develop new production and consumption networks, seeking to source local food and labour to be resilient to the risks that stem from our environmental crisis, and often forming co-operatives based on democratic principles.

For critics, these alternatives may exist for some as largely hermetically sealed enclaves that while offering moral worth, as well as pleasure, fun, and improved quality of life, achieve little in the grand scheme of things (Sharzer 2012). These are instances of 'folk politics' (Srnicek and Williams 2016) that are inward-facing, luddite and Romantic, incapable or unwilling to think systematically and towards the bigger picture (Kenis and Mathijs 2014). Fixating on the small over the big, the locally sourced over the imported, what is near-at-hand over the global – none of this makes any material difference; the argument goes, since "our problems are increasingly systematic and global and require an equally systematic response" (Srnicek and Williams 2016, 43). Indeed, development and proliferation of groups that build in the cracks, niches, and margins of globalized capitalism do not, in and of themselves, represent much of a direct competitor. It would be a mistake, however, to not see these alternatives as possessing radical transformative potential, because in doing so it would overlook the way in which the proliferation of these alternative spaces has a cumulative effect, moving the political and social status quo on a trajectory beyond globalized capitalism.

Yet they serve as 'working experiments' (Crossley 1999), places where new forms of organizing are actively developed and rolled out. For Wright (2010), the cumulative effect of these alternative forms of organizations that grow in the cracks is profound, forming an 'interstitial' mode of social transformation that seeks to erode and replace the status quo. The cumulative effect of alternative forms of organization is two-fold: their size and scope fundamentally alter the limits of what is possible, and their size and scope also pave the route to create the environment for an alternative to globalized capitalism, whatever that may be. The key point is that over time these alternative ways of living erode the conditions of possibility of the status quo, and people see their future in alternatives. Or, as Wright (2010, 334) explains, "the important idea is that what appear to be 'limits' are simply the effect of the power of institutional arrangements, and interstitial strategies have the capacity to create alternative institutions that weaken those limits". Accordingly, pursing this form of social transformation through the cumulative effect of social movements and heterodox ways of living is not so much a case of dismantling the status quo in a moment of revolutionary zeal, but rather building an alternative in the cracks of what currently exists. But is this enough?

What will emerge in globalized capitalism's wake? What lies ahead?

The global economic, social, and political fracturing has broken down any faith that globalized capitalism is operating as planned, working to the benefit of the many. Dissent and anger mean that people search for radical alternatives. What will replace globalized capitalism as the political and economic common sense remains uncertain. However, at the time of writing, the populist right that promises to remove rights and recognition for outsiders while promising a better financial future for 'natives' seems to be winning (Fraser 2019; Fraser and Honneth 2004; Rooduijn 2015). Whatever does eventually replace globalized capitalism therefore may occur within existing political and economic structures and stems from new political and economic leaders. This makes it unclear what, for definite, lies ahead.

Nevertheless, we suspect that marketing and consumer research will need to become more attuned to politics in the future. The people who we study in the future are less likely to have faith in globalized capitalism and liberal democracy. The alternatives to globalized capitalism that they seek out will require exploration, investigation, and deconstruction (Bartram 2004). As a result, the methods, concepts, and approaches marketing and consumer research has developed to analyse and take apart marketing communications can be put to work to investigate the mythmaking and storytelling of whatever political and economic common sense arises next.

It is at this juncture that it is useful to both look sideways in the broader academy as well as backwards in time and look to the future. One certainty is that marketing has been slow to engage the critical lens in comparison with other parts of the academy. This is why this book has turned the spotlight on globalized capitalism and asked readers to suspend preconceptions during reading in order to consider the five dark logics behind marketing communications. Naïve and unfounded optimism, plus inability to think about alternative modes of living, remains one of the hallmarks of the prevailing order. This book hopefully starts walking a path that will result in the flourishing of critical marketing communications (see Delbridge and Keenoy 2010).

That there is still much to do in diagnosing, interpreting, and providing ways out of our current predicament is not new. Art and music, operating in the spirit of 'Kilroy, was here', has been quick to unpack the zombie-like existence of globalized capitalism (Fisher 2018). Nonetheless, the stakes are too high to leave critique to art alone. We have sketched out conceptual and theoretical ideas here to explain how individuals and groups can reconfigure and put to work in an institutional climate that does not place value on diagnosis or critique. To move forward in this era of blunt managerial instrumentality is, of course, difficult. It is akin to the difficult act of reconciliation that existed between Jean-Jacques Rousseau and his critic, Benjamin Constant. For Constant feared the effect of Rousseau's ideas of ancient liberty would have in the modern age, believing that they would lead to political tyranny (Brint 1985). By comparison, Rousseau maintained the individual's right to pursue their own ends to the extent that these ends were limited by the laws of the general will. It is here we seem to chime with Rousseau more than Constant insofar as we see the need to reinvigorate sensitivities to the general will and public good. We also can see that the moral indeterminacy of the natural sciences alone is insufficient to help us understand the contradictions and harms that result from a world driven principally by limitless capital accumulation. The trick is for the construer to emerge 'just-in-time' (Wilkinson and Oliver 1989) and to look both backwards and forwards (Virilio 1986), to see the cracks in the sky as well as the darkness in the clouds, and to help chart potential futures outside of this social system that remains in a state of chronic disrepair.

Bibliography

Anderson, Chris (2013), *Makers: The New Industrial Revolution*, London: Random House.

Arnould, Eric J. (2007), "Should Consumer Citizens Escape the Market?" *The ANNALS of the American Academy of Political and Social Science*, 611(1), 96–111.

Arnould, Eric J. and Craig J. Thompson (2005), "Consumer Culture Theory (CCT): Twenty Years of Research," *Journal of Consumer Research*, 31(4), 868–82.

Baudrillard, Jean (1970), *The Consumer Society*, London: Sage.

Benford, Robert D. and David A. Snow (2000), "Framing Processes and Social Movements: An Overview and Assessment," *Annual Review of Sociology*, 26, 611–39.

Brint, M. E. (1985), "Jean-Jacques Rousseau and Benjamin Constant: A Dialogue on Freedom and Tyranny," *The Review of Politics*, 47(3), 323–46.

Campana, Mario, Andreas Chatzidakis, and Mikko Laamanen (2017), "Introduction to the Special Issue: A Macromarketing Perspective on Alternative Economies," *Journal of Macromarketing*, 37(2), 125–30.

Castells, Manuel (2015), *Networks of Outrage and Hope: Social Movements in the Internet Age*, Second Edition, London: Polity Press.

Crossley, Nick (1999), "Working Utopias and Social Movements: An Ivnetigation Using Case Study Materials from Radical Mental Health Movements in Britain," *Sociology*, 33(4), 809–30.

Delbridge, Rick and Tom Keenoy (2010), "Beyond Managerialism?" *The International Journal of Human Resource Management*, 21(6), 799–817.

Fisher, Mark (2018), *K-Punk : The Collected and Unpublished Writings of Mark Fisher (2004–2016)*, ed. Darren Ambrose, London: Repeater Books.

Fitchett, James A., Georgios Patsiaouras, and Andrea Davies (2014), "Myth and Ideology in Consumer Culture Theory," *Marketing Theory*, 14(4), 495–506.

Fırat, A. Fuat and Nikhilesh Dholakia (2017), "From Consumer to Construer: Travels in Human Subjectivity," *Journal of Consumer Culture*, 17(3), 504–22.

Foucault, Michel (1977), *Discipline and Punish: The Birth of the Prison*, New York: Pantheon.

——— (1980), *Power/Knowledge: Selected Interviews and Other Writings, 1972–1977*, New York: Pantheon.

Fraser, Nancy (2019), *The Old Is Dying and the New Cannot Be Born: From Progressive Neo-liberalism to Trumpy and Beyond*, London: Verso.

Fraser, Nancy and Axel Honneth (2004), *Redistribution or Recognition? A Political-Philosophical Exchange*, New York: Verso.

Godelier, Maurice (2020), *The Imagined, the Imaginary and the Symbolic*, London: Verso.

Gollnhofer, Johanna F, Henri A Weijo, and John W Schouten (2019), "Consumer Movements and Value Regimes: Fighting Food Waste in Germany by Building Alternative Object Pathways," *Journal of Consumer Research*, 46(3), 460–82.

Graeber, David (2013), "Culture as Creative Refusal," *Cambridge Anthropology*, 31(2), 1–19.

Gramsci, Antonio (1971), *Selections from the Prison Notebooks of Antonio Gramsci*, London: Lawrence and Wishart.

Greenfield, Adam (2017), *Radical Technologies: The Design of Everyday Life*, London: Verso.

Hall, Stuart (1997), *Representation: Cultural Representations and Signifying Practices*, London: SAGE.

Hill, Tim, Robin Canniford, and Peter Millward (2018), "Against Modern Football: Mobilising Protest Movements in Social Media," *Sociology*, 52(4), 688–708.

Holt, Douglas B. (2002), "Why Do Brands Cause Trouble? A Dialectical Theory of Consumer Culture and Branding," *Journal of Consumer Research*, 29(1), 70–90.

Kauffman, L. A. (2017), *Direct Action: Protest and the Reinvention of American Radicalism*, London: Verso.

Kenis, Anneleen and Erik Mathijs (2014), "(De)Politicising the Local: The Case of the Transition Towns Movement in Flanders (Belgium)," *Journal of Rural Studies*, 34, 172–83.

King, Brayden G. and Nicholas A. Pearce (2010), "The Contentiousness of Markets: Politics, Social Movements, and Institutional Change in Markets," *Annual Review of Sociology*, 36(1), 249–67.

Koopmans, R. (2004), "Movements and Media: Selection Processes and Evolutionary Dynamics in the Public Sphere," *Theory and Society*, 33(3), 367–91.

Kozinets, Robert V. (2002), "Can Consumers Escape the Market? Emancipatory Illuminations from Burning Man," *Journal of Consumer Research*, 29(1), 20–38.

Kozinets, Robert V. and Jay M. Handelman (2004), "Adversaries of Consumption: Consumer Movements, Activism, and Ideology," *The Journal of Consumer Research*, 31(3), 691–704.

Mauss, Marcel (1967), *The Gift: Forms and Functions of Exchange in Archaic Societies*, New York: W. W. Norton & Company.

McGranahan, Carole (2016), "Theorizing Refusal," *Cultural Anthropology*, 31(3), 319–25.

McLaren, Bonnie (2019), "TOWIE and Love Island Stars Agreed to Sell Lethal Cyanide Diet Drink to Their Followers," *Grazia*, https://graziadaily.co.uk/celebrity/news/lauren-goodger-cyanide/.

Murray, Jeff B. (2002), "The Politics of Consumption: A Re-Inquiry on Thompson and Haytko's (1997) 'Speaking of Fashion,'" *Journal of Consumer Research*, 29(4), 298–316.

Murray, Jeff B. and Julie L. Ozanne (1991), "The Critical Imagination: Emancipatory Interests in Consumer Research," *Journal of Consumer Research*, 18(2), 129–44.

North, Peter and Noel Longhurst (2013), "Grassroots Localisation? The Scalar Potential of and Limits of the 'Transition' Approach to Climate Change and Resource Constraint," *Urban Studies*, 50(7), 1423–38.

Oliver, P. E. and D. J. Myers (1999), "How Events Enter the Public Sphere: Conflict, Location, and Sponsorship in Local Newspaper Coverage of Public Events," *American Journal of Sociology*, 105(1), 38–87.

Ozanne, Julie L. and Jeff B. Murray (1995), "Uniting Critical Theory and Public Policy to Create the Reflexively Defiant Consumer," *American Behavioral Scientist*, 38(February), 516–26.

Rooduijn, Matthijs (2015), "The Rise of the Populist Radical Right in Western Europe," *European View*, 14(1), 3–11.

Scaraboto, Daiane and Eileen Fischer (2013), "Frustrated Fatshionistas: An Institutional Theory Perspective on Consumer Quests for Greater Choice in Mainstream Markets," *Journal of Consumer Research*, 39(6), 1234–57.

Sharzer, Greg (2012), *No Local: Why Small-Scale Alternatives Won't Change the World*, London: Zer0 Books.

Srnicek, Nick and Alex Williams (2016), *Inventing the Future: Postcapitalism and a World Without Work*, London: Verso.

Streeck, Wolfgang (2017), *How Will Capitalism End? Essays on a Failing System*, London: Verso.

Tadajewski, Mark and Douglas Brownlie (2009), "Critical Marketing: A Limit Attitude," in *Critical Marketing: Issues in Contemporary Marketing*, eds. Mark Tadajewski and Douglas Brownlie, London: Wiley, 1–28.

Thompson, Craig J., Eric Arnould, and Markus Giesler (2013), "Discursivity, Difference, and Disruption: Genealogical Reflections on the Consumer Culture Theory Heteroglossia," *Marketing Theory*, 13(2), 149–74.

Thompson, Craig J., Aric Rindfleisch, and Zeynep Arsel (2006), "Emotional Branding and the Strategic Value of the Doppelgänger Brand Image," *Journal of Marketing*, 70(1), 50–64.

Varman, Rohit and Russell W. Belk (2009), "Nationalism and Ideology in an Anticonsumption Movement," *Journal of Consumer Research*, 36(4), 686–700.

Virilio, Paul (1986), *Speed and Politics: An Essay on Dromology*, New York: Semiotext(e).

Wallerstein, Immanuel, Randall Collins, Michael Mann, Georgi Derluguian, and Craig Calhoun (2013), *Does Capitalism Have a Future?* Oxford University Press.

Weijo, Henri A., Diane M. Martin, and Eric J. Arnould (2018), "Consumer Movements and Collective Creativity: The Case of Restaurant Day," *Journal of Consumer Research*, 45(2), 251–74.

Wilkinson, Barry and Nick Oliver (1989), "Power, Control and the Kanban," *Journal of Management Studies*, 26(1), 47–58.

Williams, Raymond (1980), "Advertising: The Magic System," in *Problems in Materialism and Culture*, London: Verso, 170–95.

Wright, Erik Olin (2010), *Envisioning Real Utopias*, London: Verso.

——— (2019), *How to Be an Anticapitalist in the Twenty-First Century*, London: Verso.

INDEX

Note: **Bold** page numbers refer to tables; *italic* page numbers refer to figures and page numbers followed by "n" denote endnotes.

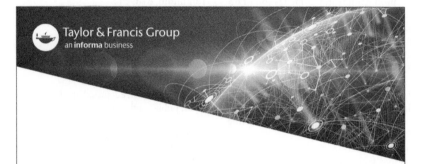